Sadlier PHONICS Reading

Level C

Lesley Mandel Morrow
Senior Author

Jane M. Carr   Emily A. Faubion   Joanne M. McCarty

Margaret M. McCullough   Lisa P. Piccinino   Diane M. Richner   Patricia Scanlon

Monica T. Sicilia   Geraldine M. Timlin   Anne F. Windle

Program Consultants

Grace R. Cavanagh, Ed.D.
Principal, P.S. 176
Board of Education
New York, New York

Ann S. Wright
Reading Consultant
Bridgeport Public Schools
Bridgeport, Connecticut

Maria T. Driend
Reading Consultant
Cooperative Educational Services
Trumbull, Connecticut

Eydee Schultz
Staff Development Specialist
Independent Consultant
Springfield, Illinois

Melanie R. Kuhn, Ph.D.
Assistant Professor of Literacy
Rutgers University
New Brunswick, New Jersey

Maggie Pagan, Ed.S.
College of Education, ESOL Specialist
University of Central Florida
Orlando, Florida

Eleanor M. Vargas, M.A.
Resource Specialist Teacher
Los Angeles Unified School District
Los Angeles, California

Frances E. Horton
Supervisor, Title I
Cabell County Public Schools
Huntington, West Virginia

Sharon L. Suskin, M.A.
Assessment Specialist
South Brunswick Public Schools
South Brunswick, New Jersey

Donna A. Shadle
Principal
St. Mary Elementary and Preschool
Massillon, Ohio

Helen Wood Turner, Ed.D.
Deputy Director of Education
Associates for Renewal in Education
Washington, D.C.

Deborah A. Scigliano, Ed.D.
First Grade Teacher
Assumption School
Pittsburgh, Pennsylvania

Sadlier-Oxford
A Division of William H. Sadlier, Inc.

Advisors

The publisher wishes to thank the following teachers and administrators who read portions of the series prior to publication for their comments and suggestions.

Margarite K. Beniaris
Assistant Principal
Chicago, Illinois

Kathleen Cleary
First Grade Teacher
Warminster, PA

Noelle Deinken
Kindergarten Teacher
Thousand Oaks, California

Susan Dunlap
Second Grade Teacher
Noblesville, Indiana

Jean Feldman
Consultant, NCEE
Brooklyn, New York

Deborah Gangstad
First Grade Teacher
Carmel, Indiana

Angela Gaudioso
First Grade Teacher
Brooklyn, New York

Sr. Dawn Gear, G.N.S.H.
Principal
Atlanta, Georgia

Mary Lee Gedwill
Second Grade Teacher
North Ridgeville, Ohio

Ana Gomez
Second Grade Teacher
Kenner, Louisiana

Patricia McNamee
Principal
Orlando, Florida

Laura A. Holzheimer
L.A. Resource Teacher, Title I
Cleveland, Ohio

Sr. Paul Mary Janssens, O.P.
Principal
Springfield, Illinois

Stephanie Wilson
Second Grade Teacher
Knightstown, Indiana

Melissa Mannetta
First Grade Teacher
Brooklyn, New York

Adelaide Hanna
Reading Resource Teacher
Brooklyn, New York

Sr. Francis Helen Murphy, I.H.M.
Editorial Advisor
Philadelphia, Pennsylvania

JoAnn C. Nurdjaja
Staff Developer
Brooklyn, New York

Mary Jo Pierantozzi
Educational Consultant
Philadelphia, Pennsylvania

Antoinette Plewa
Principal
North Plainfield, New Jersey

Pedro Rodriguez
First Grade Teacher
Los Angeles, California

Dawn M. Trocchio
Kindergarten Teacher
Brooklyn, New York

Rosemarie Valente
Second Grade Teacher
Newark, New Jersey

Earl T. Wiggins
Program Specialist, Title I
Lehigh, Florida

Acknowledgments

Special thanks to Sr. Irene Loretta, IHM, for her advice and counsel during the early developmental stages of the Sadlier Phonics program.

William H. Sadlier, Inc., gratefully acknowledges the following for the use of copyrighted materials:

"Autumn Leaves" (text only) from IN THE WOODS, IN THE MEADOW, IN THE SKY by Aileen Fisher. Copyright c 1965 Aileen Fisher. C Renewed 1993 Aileen Fisher. Reprinted by permission of Marian Reiner for the author.

"Song" (text only) from SING TO THE SUN by Ashley Bryan. Copyright © 1992 by Ashley Bryan. Used by permission of HarperCollins Publishers. Illustration by Ashley Bryan, Copyright © 1997 by William H. Sadlier, Inc.

"Sunflakes" (text only) from COUNTRY PIE by Frank Asch. Copyright © 1979 by Frank Asch. Reprinted by permission of Greenwillow Books, a division of William Morrow & Company, Inc.

"The Sidewalk Racer" (text only) from THE SIDEWALK RACER AND OTHER POEMS OF SPORTS AND MOTION by Lillian Morrison. Copyright c 1965, 1967, 1968, 1977 by Lillian Morrison. C Renewed Lillian Morrison. Reprinted by permission of Marian Reiner for the author.

"I Made a Mechanical Dragon" (text only) from THE DRAGONS ARE SINGING TONIGHT by Jack Prelutsky. Copyright © 1993 by Jack Prelutsky. Reprinted by permission of Greenwillow Books, a division of William Morrow & Company, Inc.

"Space Campers' Song" (text only) by Anastasia Suen. Reprinted by permission of the author.

ZB Font Method Copyright © 1996 Zaner-Bloser.

Product Development and Management

Leslie A. Baranowski

Photo Credits

Thomas Braise: 113 background. Myrleen Cate: 93. CO2, Inc./Christine Coscioni: 32 top, 69 center, 80 bottom, 93-94 background. Neal Farris: 17 top right, 47-48 foreground, 81-82. FPG/William McKinney: 32 center; Sebastian Starr: 117 top. John Gajda: 77. Image Bank/Bill Hickey: 94 bottom; Nino Mascardi: 48 background. Steven W. Jones: 69 top. Ken Karp: 11, 114, 151, 195, 211. Ken Lax: 97. Elyse Lewin Studio: 93. Greg Lord: 107, 117 left, 131, 155, 187, 188, 203 middle. David Mager: 34, 42. Mathison Color Photo: 36. Natural Selection: 17 top left. Photodisc/Ryan McVay: 47 music; Nick Rowe: 47 violin. Photonica/Zefa: 18 bottom left. Plastock: 203 top. Chuck Savage: 113 bottom. Stock Boston/Bob Daemmrich: 94 top. Tony Stone Images/Laurie Campbell: 18 bottom left; Don Lowe: 32 bottom. Unicorn Stock Photography/Dick Young: 69 bottom.

Illustrators

Dirk Wunderlich: Cover

Diane Ali: 34
Lisa Blackshear: 26, 60, 88, 98, 112, 125, 147, 166, 208
Joe Boddy: 8, 58, 73, 102, 140, 172
Bob Brugger: 194
Ashley Bryan: 21
Robert Burger: 40, 152, 210
Lindy Burnett: 121, 123, 130, 149
Kevin Butler: 36, 42, 95
Roger Chandler: 54, 75, 181, 195
Laura Freeman: 221, 222
Arthur Friedman: 146, 179

Adam Gordon: 30
Peter Grosshauser: 9
Debbie Haley-Melman: 78, 199, 200
Laurie Hamilton: 15, 16, 24, 28, 89, 91
Nathan Jarvis: 51, 71, 99
W. B. Johnston: 143, 182, 212
Dave Jonason: 38, 56, 61, 103, 104, 108, 135, 148, 155, 156, 201, 205, 216, 223, 224
Lauren Klementz: 90
Chris Lensch: 17, 18, 191
Andy Levine: 145, 164
Jason Levinson: 44, 63, 64, 76

Hal Löse: 5
Cheryl Mendenhall: 81, 82
Olivia: 153, 154, 163
Julie Pace: 87, 137, 138, 177, 197
Larry Paulsen: 68, 183
Jean Pidgeon: 180, 193, 211
P. T. Pie: 196, 207
Stacey Schuett: 111
Jim Starr: 165, 185, 186
Daryl Stevens: 10, 12, 70, 175
Steve Sullivan: 6, 22, 52, 86, 122, 160, 192
Richard Syska: 14

Marina Thompson: 85
Blake Thornton: 105, 159, 161, 169, 171
Brian White: 45, 46

Functional Art: Diane Ali, Sommer Keller, and Michael Woo

Contents

Autumn Leaves

One of the nicest beds I know
isn't a bed of soft white snow,
isn't a bed of cool green grass
after the noisy mowers pass,
isn't a bed of yellow hay
making me itch for half a day—
but autumn leaves in a pile *that* high,
deep, and smelling like fall, and dry.
That's the bed where I like to lie
and watch the flutters of fall go by.

Aileen Fisher

Critical Thinking

Would you prefer to lie on a bed of white snow, green grass, yellow hay, or autumn leaves? Explain your choice.

Where would you go to watch "the flutters of fall" go by?

LESSON 1: Consonants and Consonant Variants
Poetry: Rhythm and Rhyme

Dear Family,

As your child progresses through this unit about autumn, she or he will review the sounds of the consonants. The 21 letters of the alphabet that are consonants are shown below.

● Say the name of each consonant.

Apreciada Familia:

Al tiempo que los niños progresan en esta unidad acerca del otoño, repasarán los sonidos de las consonantes. Las 21 letras consonantes del alfabeto se muestran más abajo.

● Pronuncien el nombre de cada consonante.

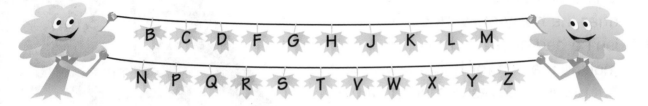

B C D F G H J K L M
N P Q R S T V W X Y Z

● Read the poem on the reverse side. Talk about the colors and smell of autumn leaves.

● Read the poem again, pausing after each pair of rhyming lines.

● See how many of the 21 consonants you and your child can find in the poem.

● Lean el poema en la página 5. Hablen sobre los colores y los olores de las hojas del otoño.

● Lean de nuevo el poema pausando después de cada par de versos.

●Miren cuantas consonantes pueden encontrar en el poema.

PROJECT

On a blank sheet of paper, list the consonants from **b** to **z**. Next to each letter, write one or two words that begin with the consonant sound. Use some of the words to write several sentences or a poem about autumn.

l leaves, listen
m maple, mowers
n nuts, nice
p pumpkin, party
q quiet
r rake, ripple
s spin
t tumble, tree

See the
maple leaves
spin in the air.

PROYECTO

En una hoja de papel en blanco hagan una lista de las consonantes de la **b** a la **z**. Al lado de cada letra escriban una o dos palabras que empiecen con el sonido de esa consonante. Use algunas de las palabras para escribir oraciones o un poema acerca del otoño.

Name _____

> **Helpful Hint** The letters **b, c, d, f, g, h, j, k, l, m, n, p, q, r, s, t, v, w, x, y,** and **z** are **consonants**.

Name each picture. Circle the consonant that stands for the beginning sound.

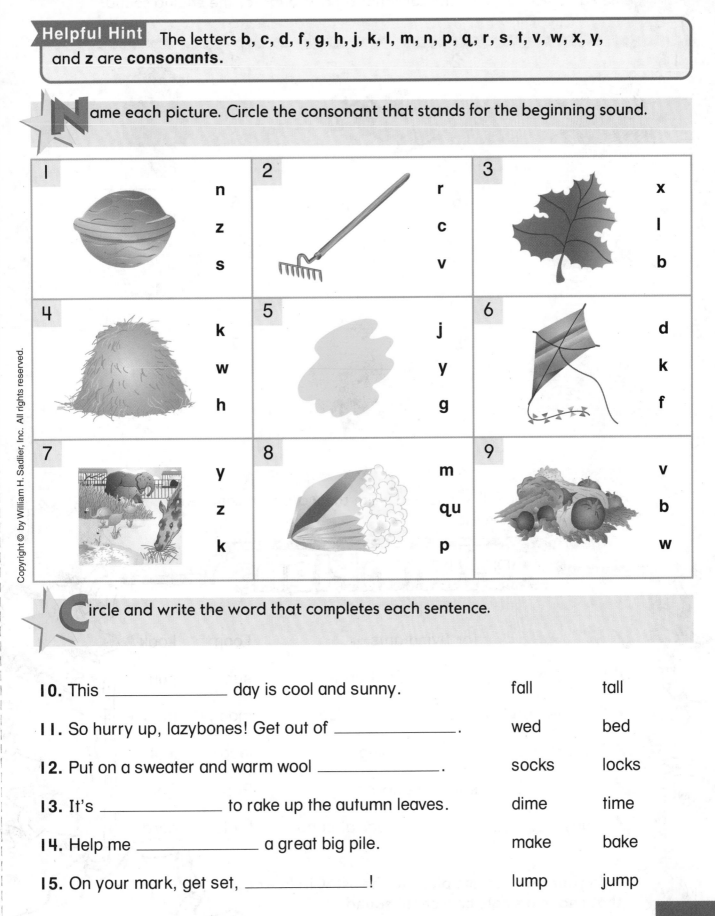

1		2		3	
	n z s		r c v		x l b
4		5		6	
	k w h		j y g		d k f
7		8		9	
	y z k		m qu p		v b w

Circle and write the word that completes each sentence.

10. This _____ day is cool and sunny.   fall   tall

11. So hurry up, lazybones! Get out of _____.   wed   bed

12. Put on a sweater and warm wool _____.   socks   locks

13. It's _____ to rake up the autumn leaves.   dime   time

14. Help me _____ a great big pile.   make   bake

15. On your mark, get set, _____!   lump   jump

LESSON 2: Recognizing and Writing Initial Consonants

7

1	2	3
4	5	6
7	8	9

Make plans for the fall. Circle and write the word that completes each item on the list.

AutumnPlans

✓ _____ for flying ants.   Loop   Look

✓ Watch the _____ set early.   sub   sun

✓ See the harvest _____ rise.   moon   moose

✓ Make a _____ rubbing.   leap   leaf

✓ _____ some popcorn.   Pop   Pod

✓ Study _____ this year at school. hark   hard

Add your own autumn plans to the list. Circle words that end in a single consonant sound.

8

LESSON 2: Recognizing and Writing Final Consonants

Ask your child to say another word that ends with the same consonant sound as each picture name in items 1–9.

Name _____

Name each picture. Write the consonant or consonants that stand for the middle sound.

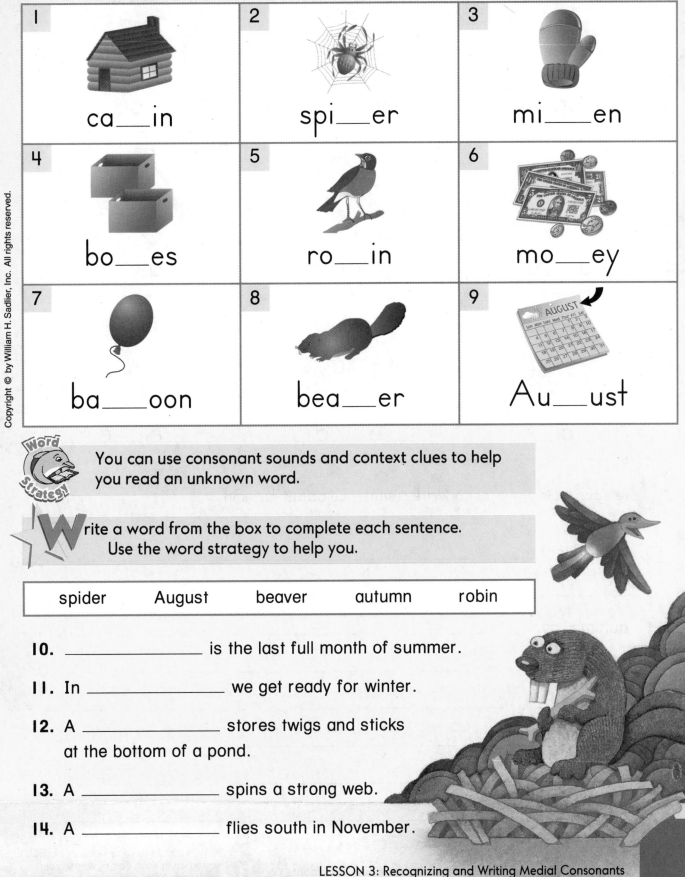

1 ca___in	2 spi___er	3 mi___en
4 bo___es	5 ro___in	6 mo___ey
7 ba___oon	8 bea___er	9 Au___ust

You can use consonant sounds and context clues to help you read an unknown word.

Write a word from the box to complete each sentence. Use the word strategy to help you.

spider	August	beaver	autumn	robin

10. _____ is the last full month of summer.

11. In _____ we get ready for winter.

12. A _____ stores twigs and sticks at the bottom of a pond.

13. A _____ spins a strong web.

14. A _____ flies south in November.

Name each picture. Write the consonants that stand for the missing sounds.

1	2	3
__oa__	__e__o__	__oo__

4	5	6
__ea__u__	__ar__	__a__o__

7	8	9
__o__	__a__a__	__e__e__

Use each pair of words to write a sentence about autumn.

10. yellow, leaf _____

_____

11. autumn, cool _____

_____

12. rake, pile _____

_____

13. wood, cabin _____

_____

LESSON 3: Reviewing Initial, Final, and Medial Consonants

Ask your child to write sentences about spring using each pair of words: **rain, mud; red, tulip;** and **robin, bunny.**

Name _____

Helpful Hint **C** usually has a soft sound when it is followed by **e, i,** or **y.** Otherwise **c** has a hard sound.

celery   cider   icy   corn

Say the words in the box. Write the soft **c** words under the picture of celery. Write the hard **c** words under the picture of corn.

icy	candle	cider	come	cones
cooks	city	slices	can't	race

1

Soft c

_____

_____

_____

_____

_____

2

Hard c

_____

_____

_____

_____

_____

Work Together

Write a word from above to complete each sentence. Then take turns reading the sentences with a partner.

3. I _____ wait to celebrate Thanksgiving.

4. My favorite cousins _____ and visit.

5. We decorate the table with pine _____.

6. Mom _____ all kinds of good food.

7. Gramps carves and _____ the turkey.

8. We all drink hot apple _____.

9. I'll _____ you to the table.

LESSON 4: Recognizing and Writing
Soft and Hard **c**

11

Helpful Hint G usually has a soft sound when it is followed by **e, i,** or **y.** The letters **dge** also have a soft sound. Otherwise **g** has a hard sound.

lar**ge**   **gi**raffe   **gy**m   we**dge**   **go**at

Say the words in the box. Write the soft **g** words under the picture of the giraffe. Write the hard **g** words under the picture of the goat.

good	budge	magic	goose	gate
guess	large	wedge	goes	gym

1

Soft g

_____

_____

_____

_____

_____

2

Hard g

_____

_____

_____

_____

_____

Write a word from above to complete each sentence.

3. Do you hear the honking? Don't _____.

4. Look up at the wild _____ overhead.

5. A wild goose is a _____ waterbird.

6. It is _____ at both swimming and flying.

7. Every fall it _____ south with the rest of its flock.

8. The flock flies in a _____, which is the shape of a **V**.

9. Can you _____ which bird is the leader?

With your child, take turns thinking of more soft **g** and hard **g** words.

Name _____

Helpful Hint **S** can stand for more than one sound.
sun   ho**s**e   ti**ss**ue

Name each picture. Circle the words that have the same **s** sound as the picture name.

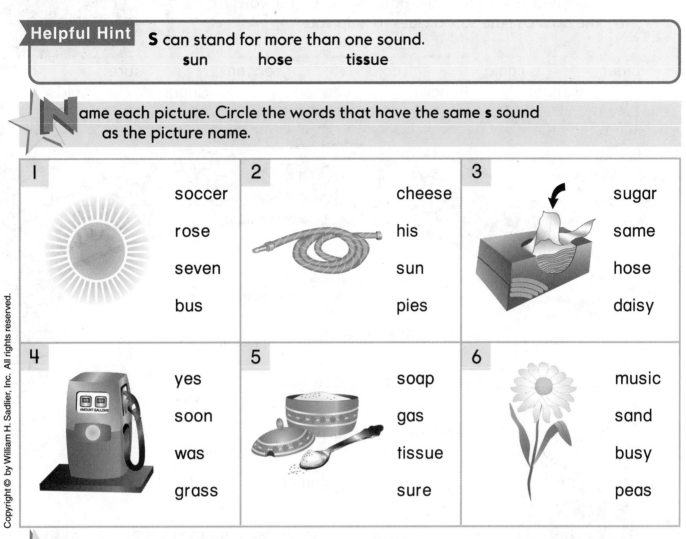

1 soccer / rose / seven / bus	**2** cheese / his / sun / pies	**3** sugar / same / hose / daisy
4 yes / soon / was / grass	**5** soap / gas / tissue / sure	**6** music / sand / busy / peas

Write the word from above that fits each clue.

7. This is a team sport played in the fall.   _____

8. This is what you use to water the garden.   _____

9. This is how you feel when you really know the answer.   _____

10. This is the number of days in a week.   _____

11. This is the sound made when you sing.   _____

12. This is what you use when you have a cold.   _____

13. This is something sweet or a kind of maple tree.   _____

Write a clue for another word that has the sound of **s.**
Exchange clues with a classmate.

Complete each line of the poem by writing a word from the box. Use the sound clues to help you.

cider	gold	cold	reason	sure
wedge	Pencils	season	Sugar	said

Best Time of Year

Autumn is my favorite _____.
(**s** in **sun**, **s** in **hose**)

Let me tell you just one _____.
(**s** in **hose**)

Even though my nose gets _____,
(**c** in **corn**)

I like leaves that turn to _____.
(**g** in **goat**)

_____ maples turn to red,
(**ss** in **tissue**)

A _____ of geese flies overhead.
(**g** in **giraffe**)

I love _____, turkey, too,
(**c** in **celery**)

_____, notebooks, all brand new.
(**c** in **celery**)

Oops! I _____ I'd tell just one.
(**s** in **sun**)

That's _____ hard. Fall's so much fun.
(**ss** in **tissue**)

Name your favorite season and write a sentence or rhyme to tell why you like it best.

Ask your child to read each sound clue and then the word he or she wrote in the blank.

Name _____

Spell, Write, and Tell

Read the phrases in the box. Say and spell each word in bold print. Repeat the word. Then sort the words according to sound and spelling. Two words can be listed under more than one heading.

yellow school **bus**

busy squirrels

old log **cabin**

tasty apple **cider**

cool fall nights

silly **goose**

large honking birds

brand new **pencil**

a good **reason**

seven days a week

sweet as **sugar**

sure about the answer

wagon for a hayride

fly in a **wedge**

c in **celery**	**c** in **corn**
_____	_____
_____	_____

g in **giraffe**	**g** in **goat**
_____	_____
_____	_____

s in **sun**	
	s in **hose**
_____	
_____	_____
_____	_____

ss in **tissue**
_____
_____

Imagine that a spaceship has landed nearby in a pile of autumn leaves. Write a paragraph in which you explain autumn to the visitors from space. Begin with a topic sentence that tells the main idea, and use one or more of your spelling words. Share your paragraph with the class.

bus	busy	cabin	cider	cool	goose	large
pencil	reason	seven	sugar	sure	wagon	wedge

All About Autumn

_____

_____

_____

_____

_____

_____

_____

_____

_____

_____

_____

_____

LESSON 6: Connecting Spelling, Writing, and Speaking

Ask your child to read his or her paragraph to you and to point out the spelling words in it.

Name _____

Read the story. Think about what happens and try to figure out why. Then answer the questions.

The Bird Feeder Mystery

It was a beautiful fall day. Bonnie looked through her window at the trees in her backyard. The leaves had changed to orange and yellow and red.

A bird feeder hung down on a string from one tree branch. Bonnie had made it from a milk carton. Many different birds were fluttering around the feeder and eating the seeds. Some seeds dropped to the ground, where a large gray squirrel gobbled them up.

Bonnie smiled, pleased that the birds liked her feeder. She turned away from the window. A moment later, she heard a noise outside. When Bonnie looked back out, the bird feeder was gone!

1. What do you think happened to the bird feeder in Bonnie's backyard?

_____

_____

2. What clue helped you figure out what happened?

_____

_____

Read and Write

Have you ever watched squirrels playing tag on a fall afternoon? Did you notice a dog or a cat watching the squirrels? Spend some time animal watching. Then record what you see. Use one or more words from the box.

Nature Notes

Word box
autumn
calm
certain
garden
gentle
huge
leaf
roam
robin
season
warm
winter

LESSON 7: Connecting Reading and Writing
Comprehension: Making Inferences

Ask your child to read his or her nature log to you. Together, add an entry to the log.

Name _____

Let's read and talk about migrating animals.

As the days in the fall get shorter and colder, many animals get ready for winter. Some store food. Others move to a different location.

Would you choose Alaska as a winter vacation spot? Bald eagles do. Every year about three thousand of them visit the state's Chilkat River. Many salmon swim there because the water is still warm. The eagles enjoy feasting on these fish.

Many other animals choose warm, sunny places. Some monarch butterflies fly to southern California in the middle of October and gather in large groups. They hang together on tree trunks or large branches and do not move again until spring.

What do you think migrating animals do in the spring?

Name each picture. Fill in the circle next to the consonant or consonants that complete the picture name.

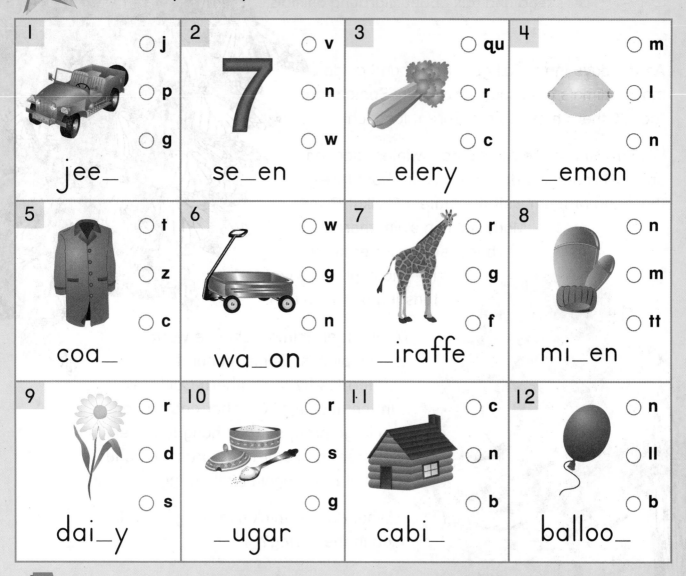

1. ○ j ○ p ○ g
jee_

2. ○ v ○ n ○ w
se_en

3. ○ qu ○ r ○ c
_elery

4. ○ m ○ l ○ n
_emon

5. ○ t ○ z ○ c
coa_

6. ○ w ○ g ○ n
wa_on

7. ○ r ○ g ○ f
_iraffe

8. ○ n ○ m ○ tt
mi_en

9. ○ r ○ d ○ s
dai_y

10. ○ r ○ s ○ g
_ugar

11. ○ c ○ n ○ b
cabi_

12. ○ n ○ ll ○ b
balloo_

Fill in the circle next to the word that makes sense in each sentence.

13. September 23 is the beginning of ___. ○ August ○ autumn

14. Each ___ day is a little shorter. ○ far ○ fall

15. The ___ sets a little earlier. ○ sum ○ sun

16. The air feels ___. ○ pool ○ cool

17. Green leaves turn ___ and red. ○ yellow ○ fellow

18. A ___ stores twigs and sticks. ○ beaver ○ beeper

19. The ___ ends in December. ○ reason ○ season

 Review this Check-Up with your child.

SONG

Sing to the sun
It will listen
And warm your words
Your joy will rise
Like the sun
And glow
Within you

Sing to the moon
It will hear
And soothe your cares
Your fears will set
Like the moon
And fade
Within you

Ashley Bryan

Critical Thinking

Why would you sing a song to the sun? to the moon?

How does the moon's response differ from the sun's response?

LESSON 9: Short and Long Vowels
Poetry: Rhythm

Name _____

Dear Family,

As your child reviews the short and long vowel sounds of **a**, **i**, **o**, **u**, and **e**, he or she will read about ways in which music enriches our lives.

- Say each word below and listen for the short or long vowel sound.

Apreciada Familia:

A medida que los niños repasan los sonidos cortos y largos de las vocales, **a**, **i**, **o**, **u**, **e**, leerán acerca de como la música enriquece nuestras vidas.

- Pronuncien las siguientes palabras y escuchen el sonido corto o largo en cada una.

short **a**	short **i**	short **o**	short **u**	short **e**
b<u>a</u>nd	d<u>i</u>sk	p<u>o</u>nd	dr<u>u</u>m	s<u>e</u>nd

long **a**	long **i**	long **o**	long **u**	long **e**
g<u>ai</u>n	f<u>i</u>ve	n<u>o</u>te	s<u>ui</u>t	f<u>ee</u>t

- Read the poem on the reverse side. Talk about "sun songs" and "moon songs."

- Read the first stanza of the poem again. Ask your child to read the second stanza.

- Look for short and long vowel words in the poem.

- Lean el poema en la página 21. Hablen de canciones acerca del sol y la luna.

- De nuevo lea la primera estrofa del poema. Pida al niño leer la segunda estrofa.

- Busquen en el poema palabras con vocales de sonidos cortos y largos.

PROJECT

Strike <u>Up</u> the (Band)

Blue <u>Skies</u>

Have a sing-along with your child. Sing a few songs. Then write down the titles or the words to the songs. Circle each word with a short vowel sound, and underline each word with a long vowel sound.

PROYECTO

Prepare una tarde de cantos junto con el niño. Canten varias canciones. Después escriban los títulos o las palabras de las canciones. Encierren en un círculo las palabras con vocales de sonido corto y subrayen las palabras con vocales de sonido largo.

Name _____

Helpful Hint If a syllable or word has only one vowel and it comes at the beginning or between two consonants, the vowel usually has the **short** sound.

h**a**t   w**i**g   c**o**t   b**u**g   p**e**n

Hat has the short **a** sound. Circle and write the short **a** word that names each picture.

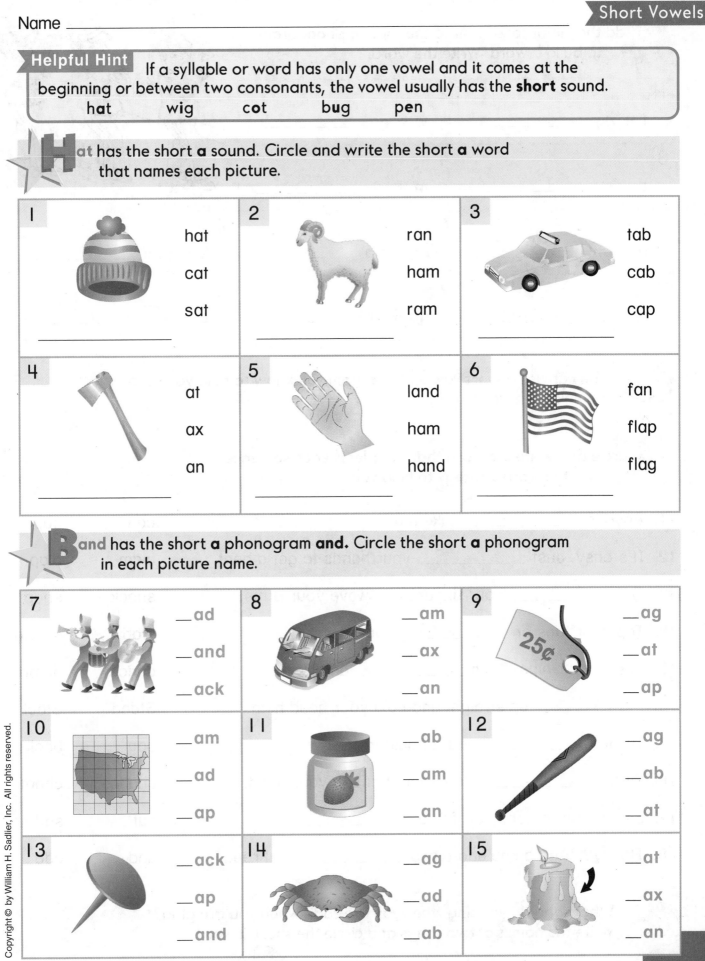

1	hat cat sat ___	2	ran ham ram ___	3	tab cab cap ___
4	at ax an ___	5	land ham hand ___	6	fan flap flag ___

Band has the short **a** phonogram **and**. Circle the short **a** phonogram in each picture name.

7	__ad __and __ack	8	__am __ax __an	9	__ag __at __ap
10	__am __ad __ap	11	__ab __am __an	12	__ag __ab __at
13	__ack __ap __and	14	__ag __ad __ab	15	__at __ax __an

LESSON 10: Short Vowel **a** Words and Phonograms

23

Add the initial consonant to the short **a** phonogram to build a word. Write the word.

1 **f** + **an** _____	2 **w** + **ag** _____
3 **c** + **ab** _____	4 **m** + **at** _____

5 **h** + **am** _____	6 **l** + **amp** _____	7 **b** + **and** _____
8 **r** + **ap** _____	9 **qu** + **ack** _____	10 **d** + **ash** _____

You can use a short vowel phonogram you know to help you read an unknown word.

Circle and write the word that completes each sentence. Use the word strategy to help you.

11. Anyone _____ make music.   can   cap

12. It's easy. Just _____ your hands to get a beat.   clam   clap

13. Or _____ your fingers and wave your arms.   snack   snap

14. Tap your toes or _____ your feet.   stab   stamp

15. Shake your hips. Then _____ and leap.   dance   damp

16. _____ up straight and hold your head high.   Stand   Stack

17. Throw _____ your shoulders.   bag   back

18. Sing or _____ the song that's in your head.   chance   chant

19. Sing if you're happy or if you're _____ .   sat   sad

20. Ready? "And a one and a two _____ a three..."   and   add

What song do you sing when you are sad? when you are glad?
Write the names of two songs and circle the short **a** words.

LESSON 10: Short Vowel **a** in Context

Ask your child to read the short **a** words he or she wrote in items 11–20.

Name _____

Wig has the short i sound. Write the short i word from the box that names each picture.

brick	crib	fin	fish	gift	lid
	list	pink	quilt	six	swim	wig

1 _____

2 _____

3 _____

4 _____

5 _____

6 _____

7 _____

8 _____

9 _____

10 _____

11 _____

12 _____

Pin has the short i phonogram in. Circle the short i phonogram in each picture name. Then write the phonogram to complete the word.

13
___im
___in
___an
p_____

14
___it
___at
___id
h_____

15
___isk
___ill
___ish
h_____

16
___ig
___ick
___ist
k_____

17
___ap
___ib
___ip
z_____

18
___ix
___ing
___ink
r_____

LESSON 11: Short Vowel i Words and Phonograms

25

Read each word. Then write a word with the same short i phonogram. Compare answers with a partner.

1 **d**ip _____	2 **k**ing _____
3 **l**id _____	4 **b**it _____
5 **d**ig _____	6 **w**ill _____
7 **t**in _____	8 **f**ish _____
9 **s**ick _____	10 **sw**im _____

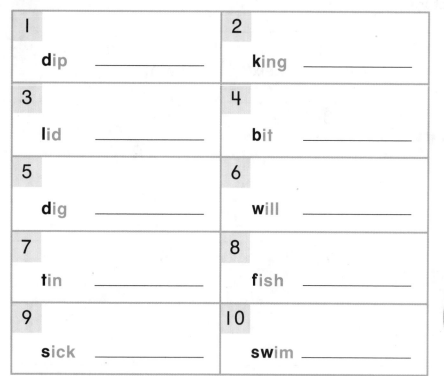

Read the poem. Underline the short i words. Then write the words below.

Whenever I hear music,
I want to sing and dance.
I can't sit still, I jump right up—
I never miss a chance.

The disk is jazz, or maybe rock—
It always makes me grin.
I feel the beat and kick my feet
And hop and twist and spin.

_____ _____ _____ _____

_____ _____ _____ _____

_____ _____ _____ _____

Write a sentence or a verse to tell what you do whenever you hear music.

Look at the words your child wrote at the bottom of the page. Together, find two pairs of rhyming words.

Name _____

Cot has the short **o** sound. Circle and write the short **o** word that names each picture.

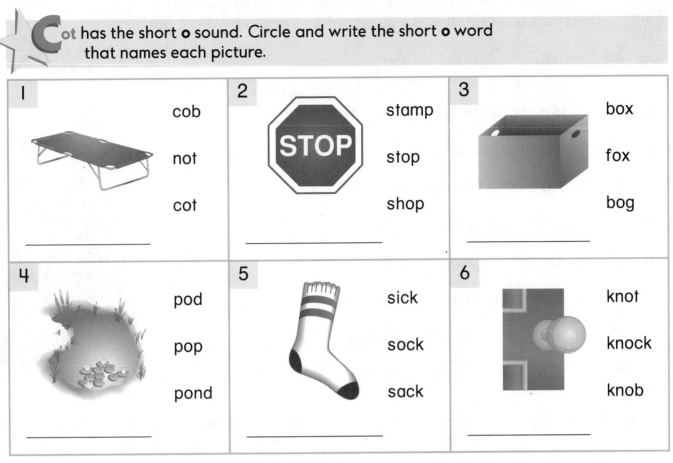

1	cob	2	stamp	3	box
	not	STOP	stop		fox
	cot		shop		bog
_____		_____		_____	

4	pod	5	sick	6	knot
	pop		sock		knock
	pond		sack		knob
_____		_____		_____	

Hop has the short **o** phonogram **op.** Say the short **o** phonogram in each picture name. Circle the words with the same phonogram.

7	top	8	dot	9	lot
	hip		hot		dock
	mop		pit		clock
	drop		pat		lick
hop		**p**ot		**l**ock	

10	hog	11	rid	12	sob
	log		cod		job
	fox		pod		cab
	jog		nod		rob
frog		**r**od		**c**ob	

LESSON 12: Short Vowel **o** Words and Phonograms

27

Write a short **o** word from the box to answer each question.
Then take turns reading the questions and answers with a partner.

cot	fox	job	jog	mop	rock	rod	stop

1. What is a piece of stone or a kind of music? _____

2. What is the opposite of **go**? _____

3. What has a bushy tail and rhymes with **box**? _____

4. What can you use to wash a floor? _____

5. What is the work a person does? _____

6. What is a pole used for fishing? _____

7. What means about the same as **run**? _____

8. What kind of bed can you fold out? _____

clock	cod	hog	hop	hot	pond	sob	sock

9. What can you do on one foot? _____

10. What do you put on before your shoe? _____

11. What means about the same as **cry**? _____

12. What has a curly tail and rhymes with **fog**? _____

13. What is the opposite of **cold**? _____

14. Where can you find fish and frogs? _____

15. What shows the time? _____

16. What is a kind of fish? _____

The bunny hop is a line dance. Think about the way other animals move and write a name for another dance. Try to use a short **o** word.

Together, think of three more short o words. Make up a question for each one.

Name _____

Bug has the short **u** sound. Write the short **u** word from the box that names each picture.

bug	bus	cut	duck	gum	mud
pup	stump	sun	trunk	tub	tug

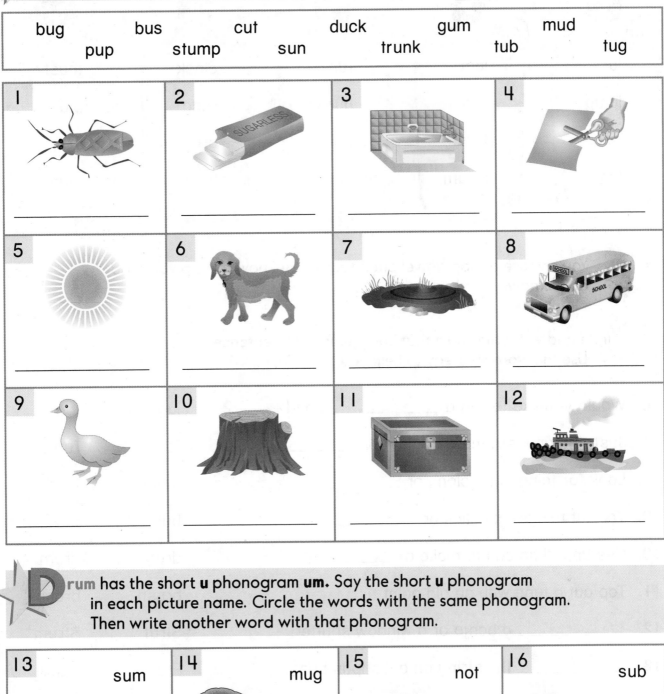

1

2

3

4

5

6

7

8

9

10

11

12

Drum has the short **u** phonogram **um.** Say the short **u** phonogram in each picture name. Circle the words with the same phonogram. Then write another word with that phonogram.

13
sum
fun
bump
plum
drum
_____

14
mug
hug
rag
dug
rug
_____

15
not
hut
shut
bun
nut
_____

16
sub
club
bud
cup
cub
_____

Circle the short **u** words.

1
luck
jump
fox
jug

2
jam
rub
twist
strum

3
fun
bunk
dance
dip

4
clock
rung
brush
thud

5
must
plus
drop
thumb

You can use a short vowel phonogram you know to help you read an unknown word.

Circle and write the word that completes each sentence. Use the word strategy to help you.

6. Would you like to join a _____ band?   jug   jog

7. Just find an instrument to play for _____.   fan   fun

8. Look for things that clang or _____.   thumb   thud

9. Try out things that click or _____.   but   buzz

10. Use an old tin can to make a _____.   drub   drum

11. Tap out a tune with an old paint _____.   brush   brash

12. _____ a banjo or a window shutter.   Strut   Strum

13. _____ the string on a dishpan bass.   Plum   Pluck

14. Pucker _____ to play a jug.   up   us

15. Invite your guests to _____ along.   hum   ham

Write a sentence or two to describe the instrument you would like to play in a jug band.

LESSON 13: Short Vowel **u** in Context

Ask your child to look at the words he or she did not circle and to say the short **u** words.

Name _____

Pen has the short **e** sound. Write the short **e** word from the box that names each picture.

belt	egg	nest	pen	pet	red	web	well

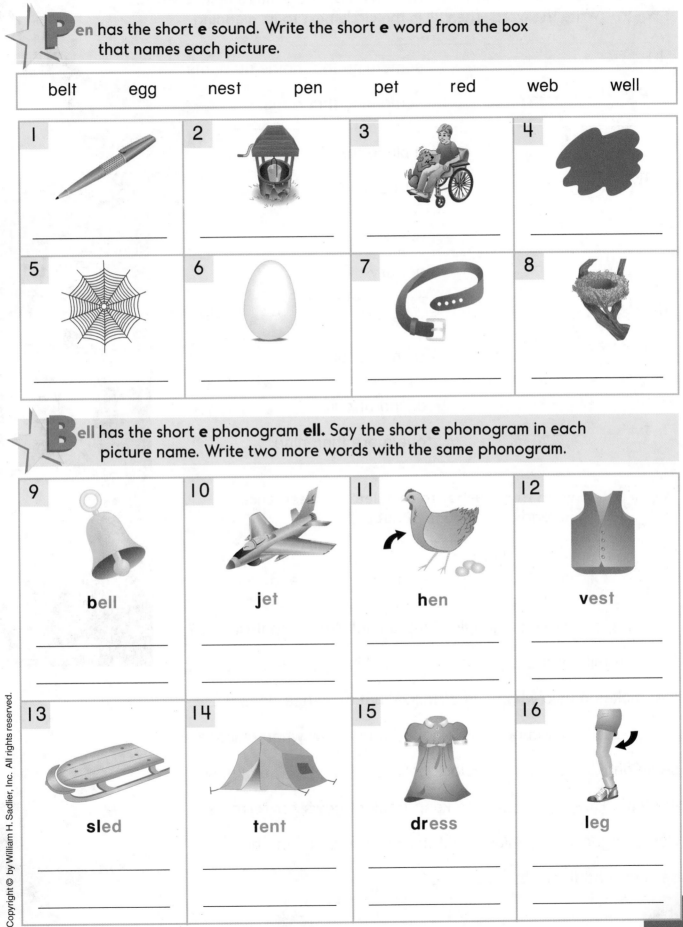

1 _____

2 _____

3 _____

4 _____

5 _____

6 _____

7 _____

8 _____

Bell has the short **e** phonogram **ell**. Say the short **e** phonogram in each picture name. Write two more words with the same phonogram.

9 **b**ell

_____
_____

10 **j**et

_____
_____

11 **h**en

_____
_____

12 **v**est

_____
_____

13 **sl**ed

_____
_____

14 **t**ent

_____
_____

15 **dr**ess

_____
_____

16 **l**eg

_____
_____

LESSON 14: Short Vowel **e** Words and Phonograms

A

Add the initial consonant to the short **e** phonogram to build a word. Write the word. Then fill in the circle next to its meaning.

1

b + ell _____
- ○ something that holds up pants
- ○ something that rings

2

n + est _____
- ○ a place for birds
- ○ a trap for fish

3

w + et _____
- ○ not east
- ○ not dry

4

c + ent _____
- ○ a penny
- ○ a small room

5

t + en _____
- ○ a kind of can
- ○ one more than nine

W

Write a word from the box to complete each sentence. Then read the selection about bells.

bell	bells	end	let
metal	necks	send	

Ding, dong! Jingle, jangle! Ding-a-ling! What's that ringing?

Can you tell it's a _____? A bell is a _____ cup

that makes music when it is struck. What message does it

_____? School bells ring to let us know when classes

begin and _____. Clock bells _____ us know

the time. Cow _____ keep track of cows for farmers.

Can you guess why mice might think it nice if all cats had

bells around their _____?

32

With your child, take turns building short **e** words by changing the first letter in **bell, nest, wet, cent,** and **ten.**

Name _____

Helpful Hint If there are two vowels in a one-syllable word, the first vowel is usually **long** and the second vowel is silent.

cake   five   rope   dune   bean

★ Look at the different spellings for long **a**.

cake   rain   jay

Circle and write the long **a** word that names each picture.

1	cake / came / cape
2	trail / tray / train
3	pay / pain / pave
4	sell / sail / sake
5	play / plate / plane
6	cage / cane / cave

★ Scale has the long **a** phonogram **ale**. Circle the long **a** phonogram in each picture name.

7	_al / _ale / _ate
8	_ate / _an / _ain
9	_ay / _ade / _ail
10	_ake / _ain / _ail
11	_ace / _ake / _age
12	_ain / _ame / _am
13	_ake / _ag / _age
14	_ay / _ail / _at
15	_al / _ale / _ate

Add the initial consonant to the long **a** phonogram to build a word. Write the word.

1 **g** + ain _____	2 **n** + ame _____
3 **w** + ay _____	4 **f** + ade _____
5 **s** + ave _____	6 **qu** + ake _____
7 **d** + ate _____	8 **n** + ail _____

Word Strategy

You can use a long vowel phonogram you know to help you read an unknown word.

Write a word from the box to complete each sentence. Then read the selection about sound.

brain	made	plays	say	shake	take	wave

How is sound _____? Let's _____

Gail sings a note. When she sings, she makes the

air vibrate, or _____. The shaking air moves

in a _____ until it reaches Jay's ear. Before

long Jay's _____ makes sense of the sound.

What if Gail _____ a violin?

When she plucks the strings, the air vibrates.

It doesn't _____ long for Jay to hear music.

Write On

Suppose a tree falls in the forest, but no one is there to hear it. Does the tree still make a sound? Write what you think.

Ask your child to sort the words in the box by spelling pattern: **a—e, ai, ay.**

Name _____

★ **L**ook at the different spellings for long **i.**
  fiv**e**   t**ie**   l**igh**t   w**i**nd
  Write the long **i** word from the box that names each picture.

| bike | five | knight | lime | pie | prize | rind | smile |

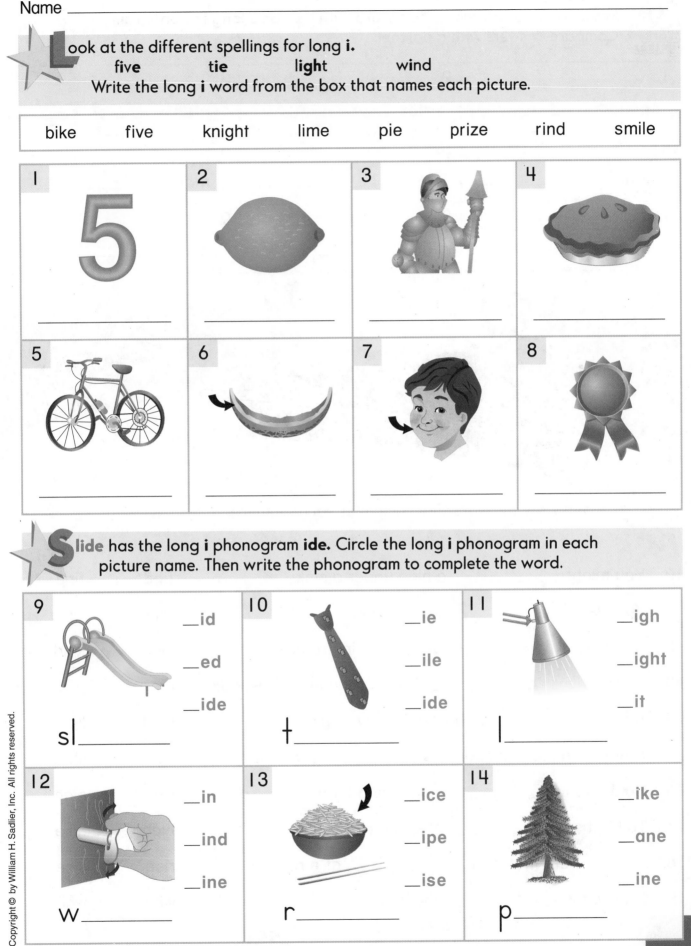

1

2

3

4

5

6

7

8

★ **S**lide has the long **i** phonogram **ide.** Circle the long **i** phonogram in each picture name. Then write the phonogram to complete the word.

9   __id
         __ed
         __ide
sl_____

10   __ie
         __ile
         __ide
t_____

11   __igh
         __ight
         __it
l_____

12   __in
         __ind
         __ine
w_____

13   __ice
         __ipe
         __ise
r_____

14   __ike
         __ane
         __ine
p_____

LESSON 16: Long Vowel **i** Words and Phonograms

35

Read each word. Then write a word with the same long **i** phonogram. Compare answers with a partner.

1 m**ind** _____	**2** r**ipe** _____	**3** n**ight** _____
4 l**ine** _____	**5** m**ile** _____	**6** n**ice** _____
7 b**ike** _____	**8** h**ive** _____	**9** p**ie** _____

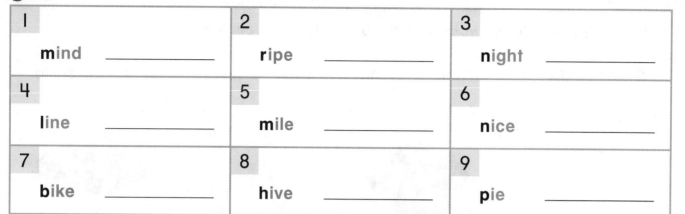

Recorder

Flute

Piccolo

Circle and write the word that completes each sentence.

10. You might _____ a pipe under a sink.   find   fine

11. You also _____ check a band.   might   right

12. A pipe is a _____ of musical instrument.   kid   kind

13. A recorder is a _____ that is made from wood.   pie   pipe

14. It is _____ to carry and easy to play.   light   lie

15. A flute is a pipe that sounds _____ a bird.   lick   like

16. Hold it to the _____ to play a tune.   ride   side

17. To hit the _____ notes, play the piccolo.   high   hike

18. It's the flute that is the _____ of a ruler.   rise   size

19. I will listen _____ you play.   white   while

With your child, look for long **i** words in a newspaper, magazine, or book.

Name _____

Look at the different spellings for long **o**.

r**o**pe   b**oa**t   sn**ow**   h**oe**   g**o**ld

Circle and write the long **o** word that names each picture.

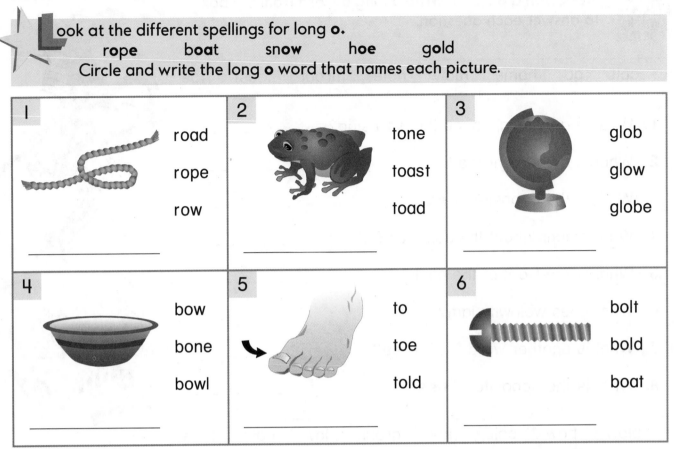

1

road
rope
row

_____

2

tone
toast
toad

_____

3

glob
glow
globe

_____

4

bow
bone
bowl

_____

5

to
toe
told

_____

6

bolt
bold
boat

_____

Cone has the long **o** phonogram **one**. Say the long **o** phonogram in each picture name. Circle the words with the same phonogram.

7

lone
man
zone
tone

cone

8

coat
bat
goat
plot

boat

9

foam
soak
glow
grow

snow

10

hole
toe
doe
toad

hoe

11

fold
sold
go
bowl

gold

12

slope
spoke
woke
soap

smoke

Work with a partner. Write a long o word from the box to answer each question.

colt	go	home	mow	note	throat	toast	toe

1. What is a musical sound that you sing? _____

2. What is a young horse? _____

3. What is the opposite of **stay**? _____

4. What means about the same as **cut**? _____

5. What is the front of the neck? _____

6. What goes well with jam? _____

7. What is another word for **house**? _____

8. What is the opposite of **heel**? _____

blow	bow	cold	doe	groan	low	pole	tone

9. What do you hear when you pick up the phone? _____

10. What is a female deer? _____

11. What is the opposite of **hot**? _____

12. What do you use for fishing? _____

13. What means about the same as **moan**? _____

14. What do you use to play a violin? _____

15. What is the opposite of **high**? _____

16. How do you play the flute? _____

Write On

Write two or three questions that can be answered with long o words. Exchange questions with a classmate.

PHONICS Alive at Home

With your child, take turns reading the questions and answers on the page.

Name _____

⭐ **L**ook at the different spellings for long **u.**
   dune   **suit**   **blue**
   Circle and write the long **u** word that names each picture.

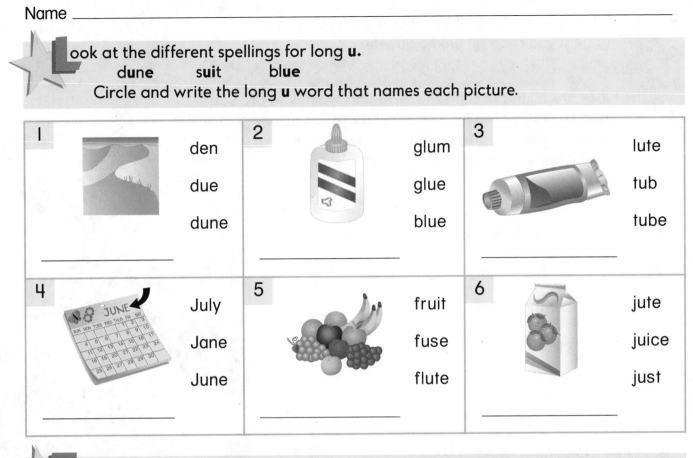

1. den / due / dune   _____

2. glum / glue / blue   _____

3. lute / tub / tube   _____

4. July / Jane / June   _____

5. fruit / fuse / flute   _____

6. jute / juice / just   _____

⭐ **T**une has the long **u** phonogram **une**. Say the long **u** phonogram in each picture name. Circle the words with the same phonogram.

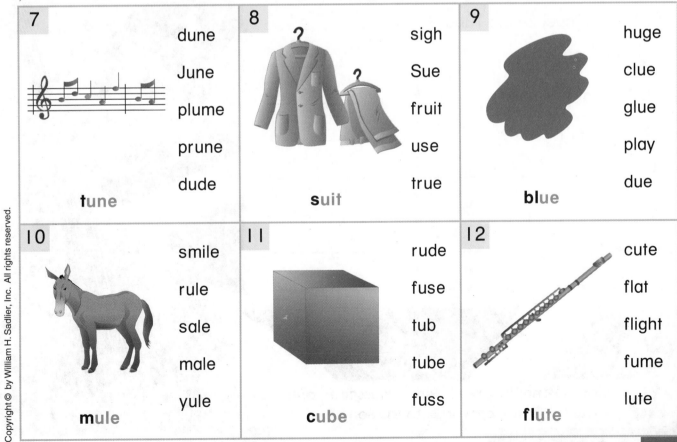

7. dune / June / plume / prune / dude   **t**une

8. sigh / Sue / fruit / use / true   **s**uit

9. huge / clue / glue / play / due   **bl**ue

10. smile / rule / sale / male / yule   **m**ule

11. rude / fuse / tub / tube / fuss   **c**ube

12. cute / flat / flight / fume / lute   **fl**ute

LESSON 18: Long Vowel **u** Words and Phonograms

39

Word Strategy You can use a long vowel phonogram you know to help you read an unknown word.

The blues are a kind of song that you sing when you are sad. Read the titles of some unusual blues songs. Circle and write the long **u** words. Then add two titles of your own to the list.

1. My Glue Won't Stick _____

2. The Runaway Mule _____

3. The Melted Ice Cube _____

4. Don't Know the Rules _____

5. Can't Keep a Tune _____

6. Can't Stand That Green Suit _____

7. Ate Rotten Fruit _____

8. Miss My Friend Sue _____

9. Don't Have a Clue _____

10. Can't Squeeze the Tube _____

11. Don't Own a Flute _____

12. My Cat Is Rude _____

13. I've Got the Blues _____

14. _____

_____

15. _____

_____

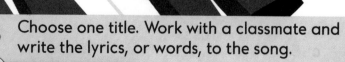

Choose one title. Work with a classmate and write the lyrics, or words, to the song.

Ask your child to use long **u** words to make up titles for songs to sing when you are happy.

Name _____

Look at the different spellings for long **e**.
bean   feet   me
Write the long **e** word from the box that names each picture.

bean   bee   green   jeep   leaf   me   peach   wheel

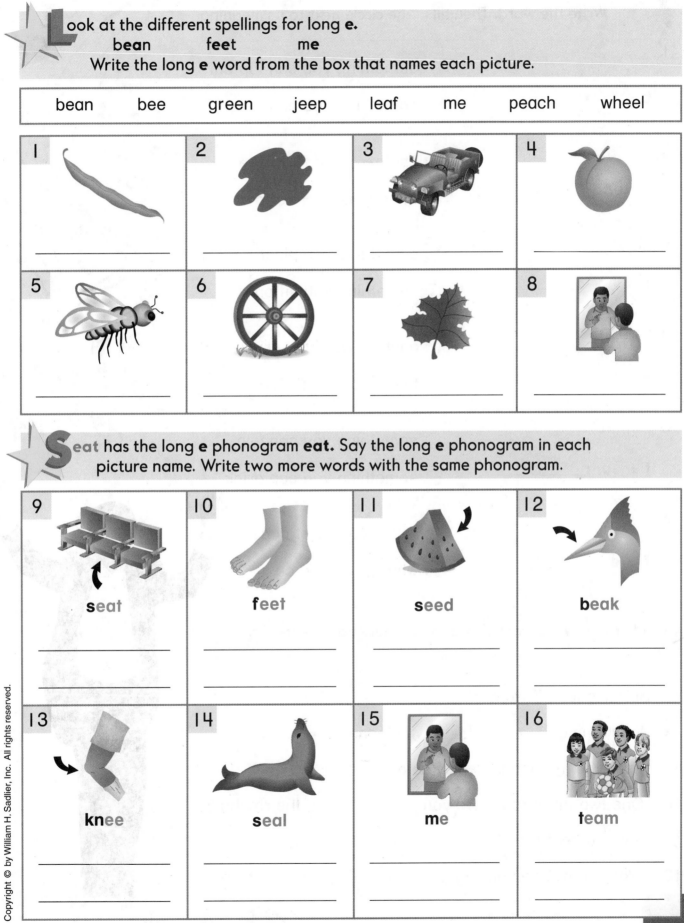

1. _____

2. _____

3. _____

4. _____

5. _____

6. _____

7. _____

8. _____

Seat has the long **e** phonogram **eat**. Say the long **e** phonogram in each picture name. Write two more words with the same phonogram.

9. **s**eat
_____
_____

10. **f**eet
_____
_____

11. **s**eed
_____
_____

12. **b**eak
_____
_____

13. **kn**ee
_____
_____

14. **s**eal
_____
_____

15. **m**e
_____
_____

16. **t**eam
_____
_____

LESSON 19: Long Vowel **e** Words and Phonograms

41

1   **b** + **eat** _____
   ○ something you can tap out
   ○ something you can see

2   **l** + **ead** _____
   ○ another word for **jump**
   ○ the opposite of **follow**

3   **s** + **eat** _____
   ○ something you plant
   ○ something you sit on

4   **k** + **eep** _____
   ○ another word for **cry**
   ○ the opposite of **give**

5   **t** + **eam** _____
   ○ something you can join
   ○ something you can drink

6   **f** + **eel** _____
   ○ what your heart does
   ○ what you stand on

★ **W**rite a word from above to complete each sentence.

7. Be my guest. Take a _____.

8. Watch me as I _____ the band.

9. I help the musicians to play as a _____.

10. "One-two-three-four." Do you _____ the rhythm?

11. Can you hear the _____?

12. Take a turn. Use your right hand to _____ time.

Ask your child to name two long **e** words that are spelled with **ea** and two that are spelled with **ee**.

Name _____

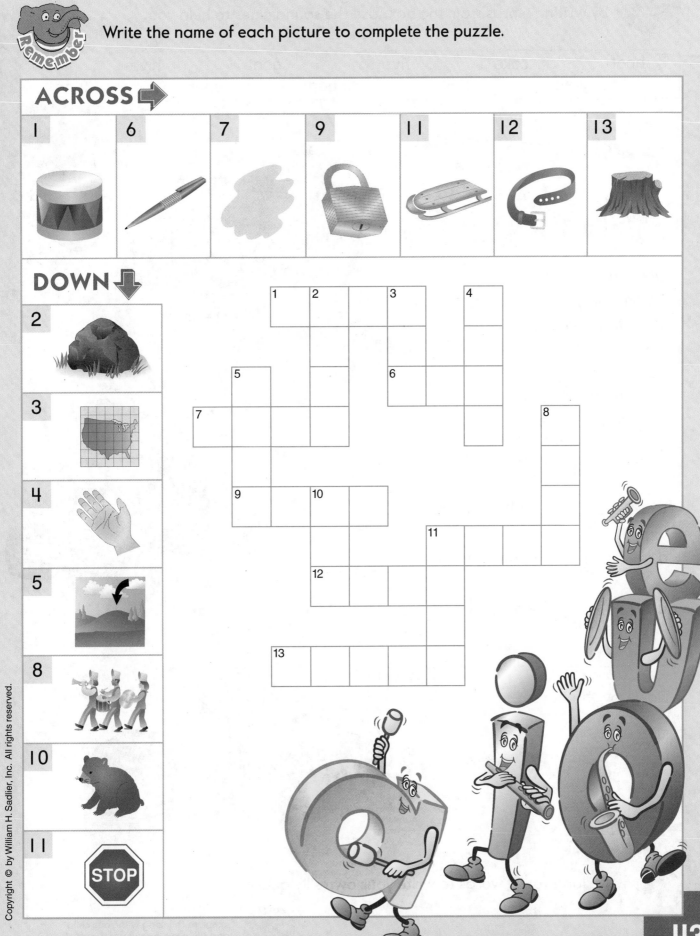

Write the name of each picture to complete the puzzle.

ACROSS ➡

| 1 | 6 | 7 | 9 | 11 | 12 | 13 |

DOWN ⬇

2

3

4

5

8

10

11   STOP

LESSON 20: Reviewing Short Vowels

43

Complete each verse of the silly song "Down by the Bay" by writing words from the box. Use the sound clues to help you.

boat	cake	five	goat	hive
jeep	mule	sheep	snake	tune

DOWN BY THE BAY

Down by the bay
Where the watermelons grow,
Back to my home
I dare not go.
For if I do,
My mother will say,
"Did you ever see . . .

a _____ eating chocolate _____?
    (long **a**)   (long **a**)

a _____ with a number _____?
    (long **i**)   (long **i**)

a _____ sunning on a _____?
    (long **o**)   (long **o**)

a _____ whistling a _____?
    (long **u**)   (long **u**)

a _____ riding in a _____?"
    (long **e**)   (long **e**)

Down by the bay.

Use long vowel words to write your own silly questions.

LESSON 20: Reviewing Long Vowels

Complete the song with your child using different long vowel words.

Name _____

Spell, Write, and Tell

Read the phrases in the box. Say and spell each word in bold print. Repeat the word. Then sort the words according to sound and spelling.

feel the **beat**
ring a **bell**
clap your hands
stamp your **feet**
hop like a bunny
hum a tune
last in **line**
hit a high **note**
turn to the **right**
shake, rattle, and roll
sing a song
wear a western **suit**
heel and **toe**
go this **way**

Short Vowels

a _____
i _____
o _____
u _____
e _____

Long Vowels

a _____

i _____

o _____
_____

u _____

e _____
_____

Spell, Write, and Tell

It's time to make music! Write a paragraph that tells how to sing a song, do a dance, or play an instrument. Use time order words, such as **first, next, then,** and one or more of your spelling words. See if a friend can follow your directions.

| beat | bell | clap | feet | hop | hum | line |
| note | right | shake | sing | suit | toe | way |

LESSON 21: Connecting Spelling, Writing, and Speaking

Ask your child to read his or her paragraph to you and to point out the time order words.

Name _____

 Read the true story about a great musician. Think about the main idea. Then answer the questions.

MOZART: The Musical Wonder Child

At age four, he played the keyboard. At age five, he began to write music. At age six, he performed for an emperor! Who is he? Wolfgang Amadeus Mozart— a musical wonder child.

Mozart was born in Austria in 1756 into a musical family. His father Leopold, a famous musician, soon became his teacher. Leopold taught young Mozart to play the harpsichord and the violin. Amazed by his son's talent, Leopold decided to go on a concert tour.

Leopold took Mozart all over Europe. The family visited Vienna, Paris, and London—all before Mozart was ten years old. On tour, Mozart played three instruments. He had his first music published, and he wrote his first opera.

As Mozart grew older, he kept writing music. He wrote over 600 pieces during his lifetime. You can still hear them today.

1. Who was Mozart's music teacher?

_____

_____

2. What was amazing about young Mozart? List two things.

_____

_____

Read and Write

Log on to a music web site, where you can share your opinions about music. Write a paragraph in which you discuss something you like or dislike. You can write about any kind of music, your favorite group or performer, the best CD or song you've heard. Use one or more words from the box.

Writer's Tips

- Start by telling what kind of music you will discuss. Tell what you like or dislike about it.
- Give at least two reasons for your likes and dislikes.

amaze

band

best

blast

dance

excite

least

music

play

rock

smile

tune

LESSON 22: Connecting Reading and Writing
Comprehension: Recognizing Main Idea and Details

Ask your child to read his or her paragraph to you. Discuss your taste in music with your child.

Name _____

 Look and Learn

Let's read and talk about a special ballet.

Have you ever seen a ballet? In this kind of performance, dancers use music to help tell a story.

The Nutcracker is one of the world's most popular ballets. The main character is a girl named Clara, who receives a gift of a wooden doll that can crack nuts with its teeth. When the Nutcracker comes alive, he and Clara have many adventures. They fight with a huge mouse called the Mouse King. Then they see dancing snowflakes. They also meet the Sugar Plum Fairy and travel to the Land of Sweets.

Are Clara and the Nutcracker's adventures real, or are they part of a dream? To find out, read the story of the Nutcracker. Or, if possible, watch a performance.

What story would you like to see performed as a ballet? Tell the story in your own words.

Fill in the circle next to the word that names each picture.

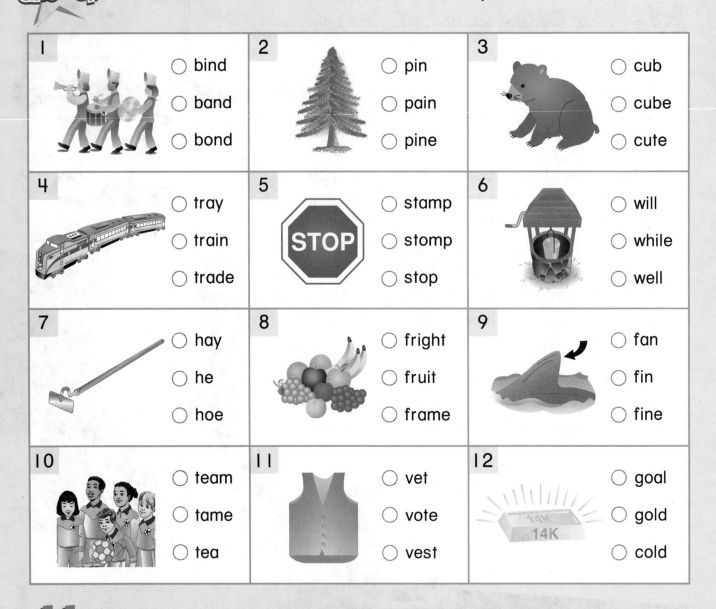

1
- ○ bind
- ○ band
- ○ bond

2
- ○ pin
- ○ pain
- ○ pine

3
- ○ cub
- ○ cube
- ○ cute

4
- ○ tray
- ○ train
- ○ trade

5 STOP
- ○ stamp
- ○ stomp
- ○ stop

6
- ○ will
- ○ while
- ○ well

7
- ○ hay
- ○ he
- ○ hoe

8
- ○ fright
- ○ fruit
- ○ frame

9
- ○ fan
- ○ fin
- ○ fine

10
- ○ team
- ○ tame
- ○ tea

11
- ○ vet
- ○ vote
- ○ vest

12 14K
- ○ goal
- ○ gold
- ○ cold

Underline each word with a long vowel sound. Then write **yes** or **no** to answer the question.

13. Can a huge whale play notes on a scale? _____

14. Is a dime the same size as a lime? _____

15. Can you bend your knees and tap your toes? _____

16. Can you squeeze a tube to get glue? _____

17. Is a green jeep the same as a red jet? _____

18. Can you use a mug to drink milk with a meal? _____

 Review this Check-Up with your child.

Read Aloud

Sunflakes

If sunlight fell like snowflakes,
gleaming yellow and so bright,
we could build a sunman,
we could have a sunball fight,
we could watch the sunflakes
drifting in the sky.
We could go sleighing
in the middle of July
through sundrifts and sunbanks,
we could ride a sunmobile,
and we could touch sunflakes—
I wonder how they'd feel.

Frank Asch

Critical Thinking

If sunlight fell like snowflakes, what would you do?

If you could touch sunflakes, how do you think they would feel?

LESSON 24: Syllables, Consonant Blends, Compound Words,
y as a Vowel, and Consonant Digraphs
Poetry: Rhythm and Rhyme

51

Name _____

Dear Family,

In this unit your child will use his or her imagination while learning phonics skills. Share these definitions:

consonant blend: two or three consonants sounded together so that each letter is heard (**cl**oud, ne**st**)

compound word: new word made up of two or more smaller words (**sunlight**)

words with y as a vowel: words in which **y** has the sound of long **i** or long **e** (sh**y**, part**y**)

consonant digraph: two consonants together that stand for one sound (**th**ink, wi**sh**)

• Read the poem on the reverse side, pausing after each pair of lines to emphasize the rhyming words. Talk about what would happen if sunlight fell like snowflakes.

• Look in the poem for examples of consonant blends, compound words, words with **y** as a vowel, and consonant digraphs.

PROJECT

Make a list of compound words. Then write each word part on an index card. Shuffle the cards and pick two at random to make a new compound word. Use the word in a silly sentence.

Apreciada Familia:

En esta unidad los niños usarán la imaginación mientras aprenden destrezas fonéticas. Compartan estas definiciones:

mezcla de consonantes: dos o tres consonantes suenan juntas en una palabra de tal forma que cada una se puede oír (**cl**oud, ne**st**)

palabras compuestas: palabra nueva formada por dos o más palabras (**sunlight**)

y con sonido de vocal: palabras donde la **y** tiene el sonido largo de la **i** o la **e** (sh**y**, part**y**)

consonantes dígrafas: dos consonantes juntas que producen un solo sonido (**th**ink, wi**sh**)

• Lea el poema en la página 51 pausando después de cada par de versos para reforzar las palabras rítmicas. Hablen de lo que pasaría si la luz solar cayera como copos de nieve.

• Busquen ejemplos en el poema de mezcla de consonantes, palabras compuestas, palabras donde la **y** tiene sonido vocal y consonantes dígrafas.

PROYECTO

Hagan una lista de palabras compuestas. Escriban las partes de las palabras en una tarjeta 3 X 5. Barajen las tarjetas y saquen dos para formar una nueva palabra compuesta con ellas. Usen la palabra en una oración tonta.

sunshine
strawberry
wishbone
butterfly

wish berry

Name _____

Every **syllable** has a vowel sound. Words can have one or more syllables.
lemon—**2** vowel sounds—**2** syllables

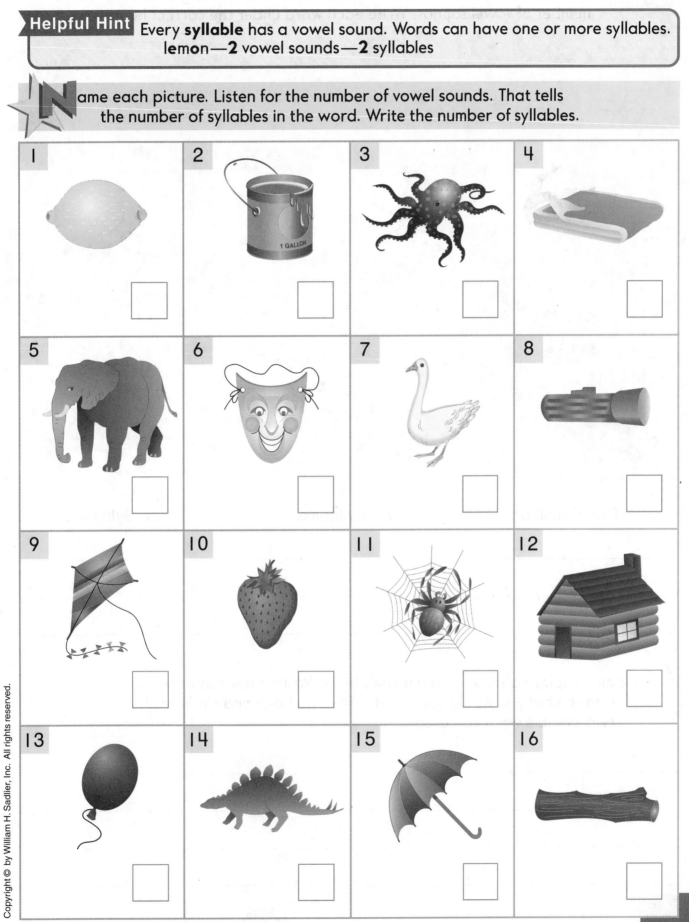

Name each picture. Listen for the number of vowel sounds. That tells the number of syllables in the word. Write the number of syllables.

1

2   1 GALLON

3

4

5

6

7

8

9

10

11

12

13

14

15

16

What can be seen under the sea? Say the name of each thing and listen for the number of vowel sounds. Write each word under the correct heading.

jellyfish

eel

angelfish

crab

octopus

turtle

sponge

lobster

seaweed

One Syllable	Two Syllables	Three Syllables
_____	_____	_____
_____	_____	_____
_____	_____	_____

Imagine exploring the sea on a turtle's back. Write a few sentences about what you would see and do. Then go back and circle each two-syllable word you used.

_____

_____

_____

_____

LESSON 25: Recognizing Syllables

Name _____

Helpful Hint A **consonant blend** is two or three consonants sounded together so that each letter is heard.

cloud　　　twig　　　drum　　　snow　　　nest

Circle the blend that begins each picture name. Then write the **l**-blend or **tw** to complete the word.

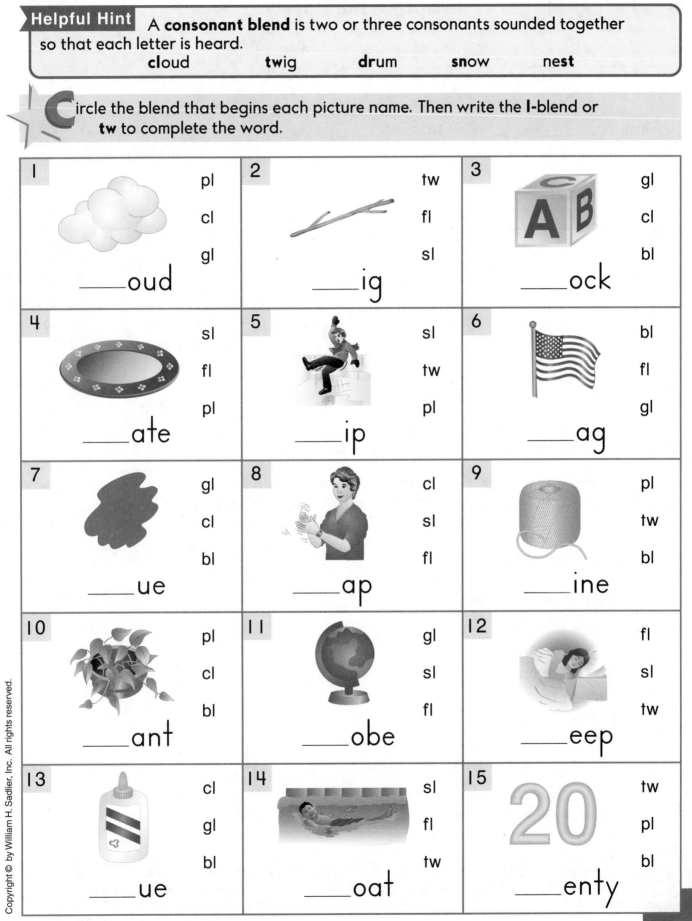

1. pl cl gl ___oud
2. tw fl sl ___ig
3. gl cl bl ___ock
4. sl fl pl ___ate
5. sl tw pl ___ip
6. bl fl gl ___ag
7. gl cl bl ___ue
8. cl sl fl ___ap
9. pl tw bl ___ine
10. pl cl bl ___ant
11. gl sl fl ___obe
12. fl sl tw ___eep
13. cl gl bl ___ue
14. sl fl tw ___oat
15. tw pl bl ___enty

Read each word. Then write a word with the same phonogram. Begin the new word with a blend from the box.

bl	cl	fl	gl	pl	sl	tw

1 **s**ock _____	2 **t**ub _____
3 **b**at _____	4 **d**ig _____
5 **r**ed _____	6 **n**ame _____
7 **h**ide _____	8 **r**obe _____
9 **t**eam _____	10 **g**ate _____

Read the poem. Underline the words that begin with **l**-blends or **tw.** Then write each word next to its beginning blend.

imagine

A cloud is anything
I want it to be—
A plate or a glider,
What else can I see?
A sleek flying saucer
Twirling towards me.

cl _____ fl _____ gl _____

pl _____ sl _____ tw _____

Use your imagination. Write a poem about something you see in the clouds. Use at least one word that begins with an **l**-blend or **tw.**

Together, think of another word that begins with each blend in the box at the top of the page.

Drum begins with the **r-blend dr.** Write an **r-blend** from the box to complete each picture name.

br	cr	dr	fr	gr	pr	tr

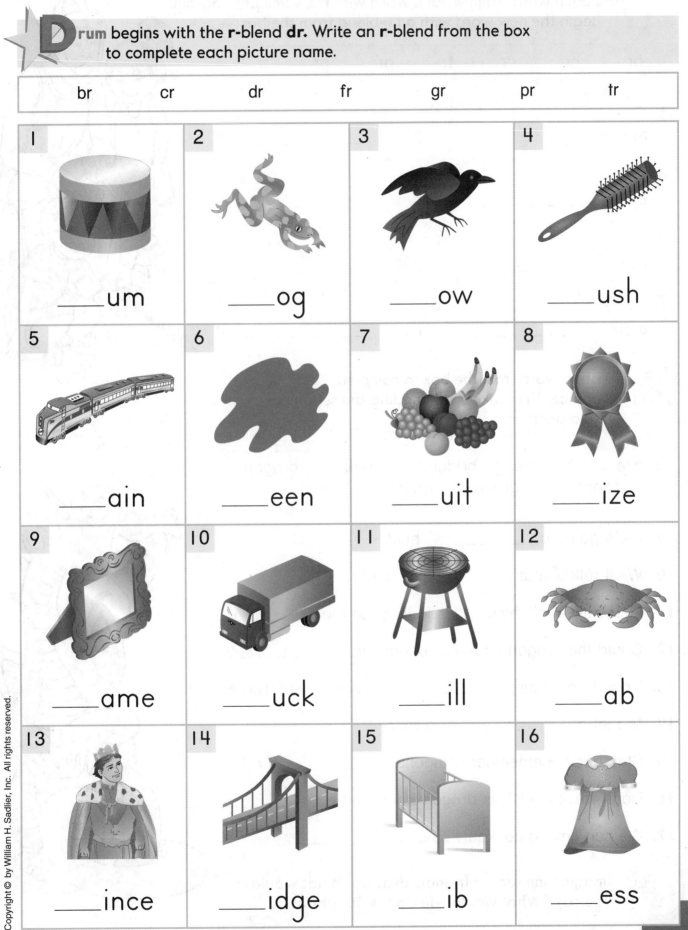

1 ____um

2 ____og

3 ____ow

4 ____ush

5 ____ain

6 ____een

7 ____uit

8 ____ize

9 ____ame

10 ____uck

11 ____ill

12 ____ab

13 ____ince

14 ____idge

15 ____ib

16 ____ess

Read each word. Then write a word with the same phonogram. Begin the new word with an **r**-blend from the box.

br	cr	dr	fr	gr	pr	tr

1 **m**ess _____	2 **l**ight _____
3 **b**ack _____	4 **s**ay _____
5 **l**ow _____	6 **h**ill _____
7 **c**ave _____	8 **r**ide _____

Write a word from the box to complete each sentence. Then take turns reading the sentences with a partner.

brave	breathe	bridge	creek	dragon

friend	green	groan	treat

9. Let's go on a _____ hunt.

10. We'll follow that _____ knight.

11. Looks like we'll have to wade through the _____.

12. Could the dragon be hiding under the _____?

13. I don't see a large _____ creature with red wings!

14. Is that a _____ or a roar?

15. Step back. Remember, dragons _____ fire!

16. Don't run away! This dragon wants to be our _____.

17. We can have a cookout. What a _____!

Imagine meeting a friendly dragon. What would you say? What would you do? Write about it.

LESSON 27: Initial **r**-blends in Context

Use three words with **r**-blends in a sentence, for example: The **dragon** under the **bridge breathes** fire.

Name _____

Snow begins with the **s**-blend **sn.** Each word in the box begins with an **s**-blend. Write the word that names each picture.

snow	spill	scale	scarf	screw	smile	snake	store
sky	stove	spoon	spring	street	square	swing	swan

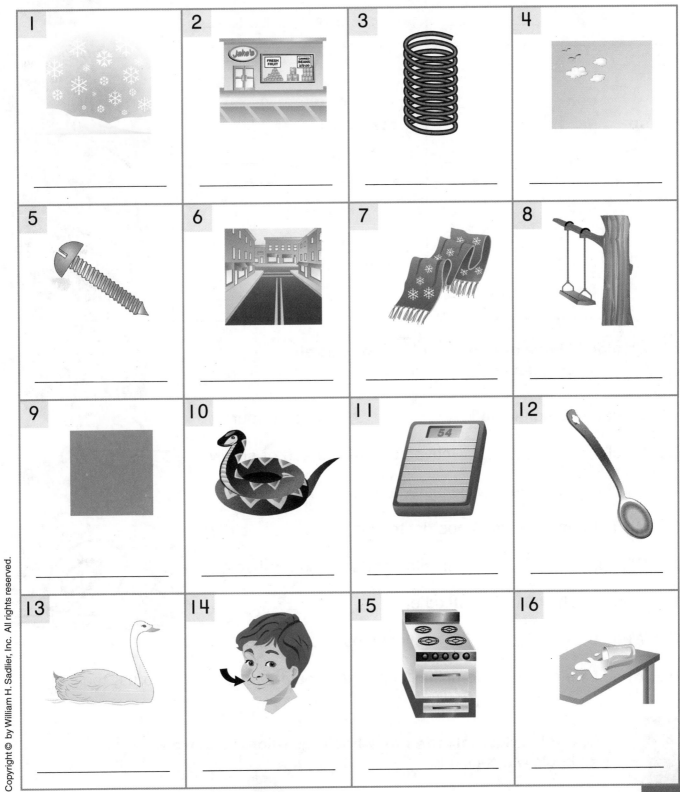

1 _____

2 _____

3 _____

4 _____

5 _____

6 _____

7 _____

8 _____

9 _____

10 _____

11 _____

12 _____

13 _____

14 _____

15 _____

16 _____

Circle two phonograms that can be added to each **s**-blend to form a word. Write the words.

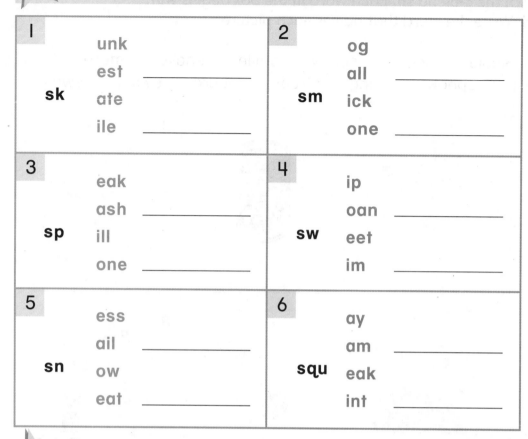

1			2		
	unk			og	
	est	_____		all	_____
sk	ate		**sm**	ick	
	ile	_____		one	_____

3			4		
	eak			ip	
	ash	_____		oan	_____
sp	ill		**sw**	eet	
	one	_____		im	_____

5			6		
	ess			ay	
	ail	_____		am	_____
sn	ow		**squ**	eak	
	eat	_____		int	_____

What if? Write a word from above to complete each question.

7. What if a lemon tasted _____ instead of sour?

8. What if a _____ moved quickly instead of slowly?

9. What if an ant were large instead of _____?

10. What if a mouse said "moo" instead of "_____"?

11. What if a _____ smelled good instead of bad?

12. What if fish could fly instead of _____?

13. What if _____ fell in sheets instead of flakes?

14. What if we could talk to animals and they could _____ to us, too?

Work with a classmate to write "what if" questions using words that begin with **s**-blends.

Take turns reading the questions above with your child.

Name _____

Nest ends with the consonant blend **st**. Circle the blend that ends each picture name. Write the word.

1	ft / ng / st	2	lt / mp / ld	3	lf / nt / nk
4	mp / lt / st	**5**	nd / lf / mp	**6**	nd / ft / nk
7	nd / st / ld	**8**	nt / ng / mp	**9**	nk / lt / nd

Write a word from the box to complete each sentence.

camp	gold	left	nest	sound	tent

10. We like to _____ out in the woods.

11. Our _____ is safe and warm.

12. One night we heard a loud squawking _____.

13. We _____ our cots to follow the noise.

14. We found a huge _____ hidden in some tall grass.

15. There were two shiny _____ eggs inside.

Write on

What do you think happened next? Write about it.
Share your story ending with classmates.

You can use a syllable you know to help you read an unknown word.

cat   **clat**ter   **flat**ter   **plat**ter   **scat**ter

Say each syllable. Then combine the syllables to write a word.

1

clat + ter   _____

flat + ter   _____

plat + ter   _____

scat + ter   _____

2

squeak + y   _____

sneak + y   _____

creak + y   _____

streak + y   _____

3

play + ing   _____

stay + ing   _____

spray + ing   _____

bray + ing   _____

4

land + ed   _____

hand + ed   _____

sand + ed   _____

brand + ed   _____

Work Together

**Write the two-syllable word from above that fits each clue.
Compare answers with a partner.**

5. It begins with **clat.**
It's another word for **noise.**

The word is _____ .

6. It begins with **stay.**
It's the opposite of **going.**

The word is _____ .

7. It begins with **creak.**
It describes a door that needs oil.

The word is _____ .

8. It begins with **hand.**
It's another word for **gave.**

The word is _____ .

9. It begins with **sand.**
It means "made smooth."

The word is _____ .

10. It begins with **plat.**
It's a large dish.

The word is _____ .

Together, write a riddle for each of the following words: **flatter, squeaky, playing, landed.**

Name _____

Read the phrases in the box. Say and spell each word in bold print. Repeat the word. Then sort the words according to sound and spelling. Some words can be listed under more than one heading.

bring a gift	
not a **cloud** in the sky	
something to **drink**	
a good **friend**	
a **gleam** in her eye	
hold on tight	
left it behind	
water the **plant**	
visit the duck **pond**	
a friendly **smile**	
spill the milk	
swing to and fro	
try your best	
twice as nice	

l-blend
_____
_____
_____

tw
_____

r-blend
_____
_____
_____
_____

s-blend
_____
_____

Final Blend
_____
_____
_____
_____
_____
_____

Spell Write, and Tell

Take the part of a spider. Imagine that you've just finished spinning a web. Write a note inviting a fly to join you there. In your note, use one or more of your spelling words. Send the note to a friend.

bring	cloud	drink	friend	gleam	hold	left
plant	pond	smile	spill	swing	try	twice

heading → _____

_____

_____

Dear _____ , ← greeting

← body

_____

_____

_____

_____

_____

_____

_____

_____

_____

closing → _____

signature → _____

LESSON 31: Connecting Spelling, Writing, and Speaking

PHONICS Alive at Home Ask your child to read his or her note to you and to point out the five parts that are labeled.

Name _____

Learn how to make paint blots. Complete each sentence by writing a word from the box. Use the sound clues to help you.

blot	clown	Drip	Fold	friend	list
paint	Press	spot	spread	try	twig

1. Here is an art activity you can _____.
   (**r**-blend)

2. Get a jar of _____ and some paper.
   (final blend)

3. _____ the paper in half. Open it.
   (final blend)

4. _____ a few drops of paint inside along the fold.
   (**r**-blend)

5. Refold the paper. _____ down outside along the fold.
   (**r**-blend)

6. As you press, the paint will _____.
   (**s**-blend)

7. Open the paper and look carefully at the paint _____ you've made.
   (**l**-blend)

8. Use your imagination, and it's more than a _____!
   (**s**-blend)

9. Is it a _____ wearing a bow tie?
   (**l**-blend)

10. Or is it a butterfly resting on a _____?
    (**tw**)

11. Make a _____ of all the things it could be.
    (final blend)

12. Ask a _____ what he or she sees.
    (**r**-blend, final blend)

Check-Up Write the word that names each picture. Circle the consonant blend at the beginning or end of the picture name.

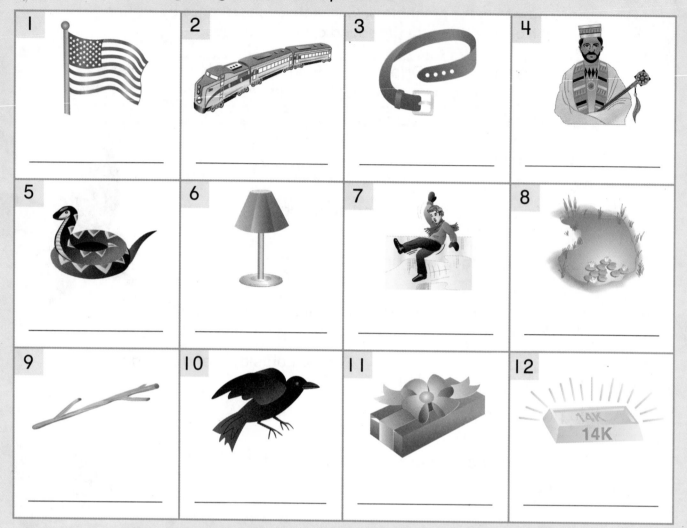

1	2	3	4
_____	_____	_____	_____

5	6	7	8
_____	_____	_____	_____

9	10	11	12
_____	_____	_____	_____

Circle the word that fits each clue.

13. This is used for cooking or heating.	store	grove	stove
14. This is another word for **noise.**	cloud	sound	found
15. This is where birds lay eggs.	nest	vest	tent
16. This strong string can be used to tie boxes.	twine	spine	swine
17. This word goes with **ice.**	snail	snow	stow
18. This is used to stick things together.	blue	glue	clue
19. This is used for cooking or broiling.	drill	skill	grill
20. This instrument makes a sound when you beat it.	plum	drum	spun

Name _____

Helpful Hint   A **compound word** is made up of two or more smaller words.
wish + bone = wishbone

Combine two words from the box to name each picture.
Write each compound word.

back	ball	bone	box	coat	corn	foot	lace
mail	mill	pack	pop	rain	shoe	wind	wish

1. _____

2. _____

3. _____

4. _____

5. _____

6. _____

7. _____

8. _____

Work Together   Write a compound word from above for each definition. Then take turns reading the definitions and compound words with a partner.

9. This is a ball you kick with your foot.   _____

10. This is a bone you make a wish on.   _____

11. This is a lace used to tie a shoe.   _____

12. This is a coat that protects you from rain.   _____

13. This is corn that pops when it is heated.   _____

14. This is a mill that is worked by the wind.   _____

15. This is a pack you wear on your back.   _____

16. This is a box in which you mail letters.   _____

A Add a word from the box to each word to form a compound word. Write the compound word.

| cut | flake | fruit | hive | lid |
| side | stairs | time | way | work |

1	snow _____	2	hill _____
3	hair _____	4	bed _____
5	grape _____	6	home _____
7	eye _____	8	up _____
9	drive _____	10	bee _____

You can use a syllable or small word you know to help you read a compound word.

R Read each sentence and circle the compound word. Use the word clues to help you.

rain 11. What kind of flakes would fall from a rainbow?

box 12. Look what I found in my mailbox!

pan 13. Why is our kitchen filled with pancakes?

ship 14. Is that a spaceship in the yard?

fish 15. That is the strangest goldfish I've ever seen!

play 16. Did you ever have a make-believe playmate?

horse 17. Who rode to school on horseback?

play 18. Have you seen the playground of the future?

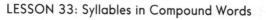

How many compound words can you make by adding a word after **snow**? before **ball**? Make a list with a classmate.

With your child, take turns making up definitions for the compound words circled in items 11–18.

Name _____

Helpful Hint **Y** usually has the long **i** sound when it is the only vowel at the end of a one-syllable word. When **y** is the only vowel at the end of a word with more than one syllable, it usually has the long **e** sound.

   fly—**1** syllable—long **i**   baby—**2** syllables—long **e**

Say the words in the box. Write the words in which **y** has the long **i** sound under the picture of the fly. Write the words in which **y** has the long **e** sound under the picture of the baby.

by	cry	daisy	jelly	muddy
my	penny	puppy	sky	spy

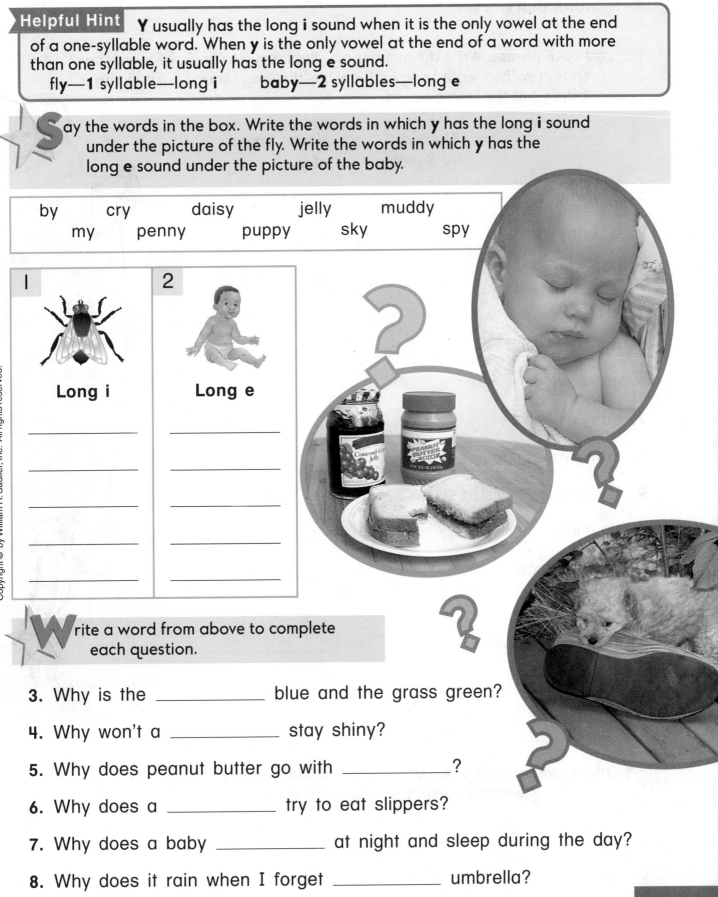

1   Long i

_____
_____
_____
_____
_____

2   Long e

_____
_____
_____
_____
_____

Write a word from above to complete each question.

3. Why is the _____ blue and the grass green?

4. Why won't a _____ stay shiny?

5. Why does peanut butter go with _____?

6. Why does a _____ try to eat slippers?

7. Why does a baby _____ at night and sleep during the day?

8. Why does it rain when I forget _____ umbrella?

You can use what you know about syllables to help you read words that end in **y.**

Read each phrase. Write the number of syllables you hear in the word that ends in **y.** Then write **Long i** if the **y** has the long **i** sound. Write **Long e** if the **y** has the long **e** sound.

	Number of Syllables	Vowel Sound of **y**
1. ask **why**	____	_____
2. a **funny** joke	____	_____
3. a **happy** smile	____	_____
4. **sly** as a fox	____	_____
5. **my** best friend	____	_____
6. go **slowly**	____	_____
7. **easy** as can be	____	_____
8. **many** years ago	____	_____
9. **fry** an egg	____	_____
10. **fly** a kite	____	_____
11. a **pretty** face	____	_____
12. on **dry** land	____	_____
13. **carry** an umbrella	____	_____
14. **try** harder	____	_____
15. a **lucky** day	____	_____

Write a sentence using two or more words that end in **y.** Then go back and circle each two-syllable word that ends in **y.**

_____

_____

LESSON 34: Syllables in Words with **y** as a Vowel

Together, look for words with **y** as a vowel in a newspaper, magazine, or book. Say the words.

Name _____

Write a word from the box for each clue. Then read down to find the answer to the question.

bedtime	dry	earmuffs	easy	fly	inside	mailbox
popcorn	raindrop	rainy	sky	snowflake	sunny	windy

1. a drop of rain __ __ __ __ __ __ __ __

2. having much wind __ __ __ __ __

3. not wet __ __ __

4. muffs, or coverings, for the ears __ __ __ __ __ __ __ __

5. having much rain __ __ __ __ __

6. what you see above you outside __ __ __

7. having much sunshine __ __ __ __ __

8. a flake of snow __ __ __ __ __ __ __ __ __

9. a box for mail __ __ __ __ __ __ __

10. corn that pops __ __ __ __ __ __ __

11. time for bed __ __ __ __ __ __ __

12. the side that is in __ __ __ __ __ __

13. what a bird does __ __ __

14. not hard __ __ __ __

What can you do during a sunstorm?

_____

How many words can you make by adding a small word or **y** to **rain** or **snow**? Work with a classmate to make a list.

Check-Up Fill in the circle next to the word that completes each compound word. Write the compound word.

1		2		3	
wish____	○ house ○ bone ○ fall	bed____	○ time ○ dream ○ rise	ear ____	○ cakes ○ hive ○ muffs
_____		_____		_____	

4		5		6	
rain____	○ wet ○ over ○ coat	shoe____	○ chair ○ lace ○ way	in____	○ side ○ time ○ sun
_____		_____		_____	

7		8		9	
foot____	○ ball ○ side ○ bow	mail____	○ clock ○ way ○ box	snow____	○ rain ○ flake ○ coin
_____		_____		_____	

10		11		12	
back____	○ lid ○ pack ○ fish	grape____	○ mate ○ cut ○ fruit	space____	○ drop ○ mill ○ ship
_____		_____		_____	

Write **i** beside each word in which **y** has the long **i** sound. Write **e** beside each word in which **y** has the long **e** sound.

13. baby ____	**14.** penny ____	**15.** by ____	**16.** shiny ____
17. dry ____	**18.** why ____	**19.** daisy ____	**20.** sky ____
21. fly ____	**22.** try ____	**23.** my ____	**24.** jelly ____
25. muddy ____	**26.** cry ____	**27.** carry ____	**28.** lucky ____

LESSON 35: Assessing Compound Words and **y** as a Vowel

Review this Check-Up with your child.

Name _____

Helpful Hint A **consonant digraph** is two consonants together that stand for one sound.

think   clo**ck**   di**sh**es

Circle the consonant digraph that begins each picture name. Then write the digraph to complete the word.

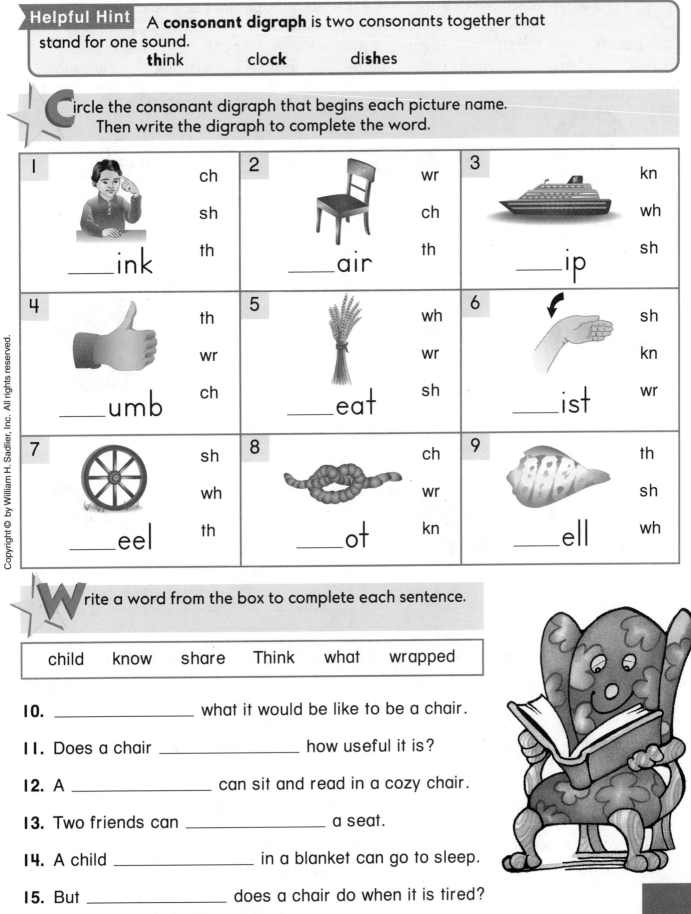

1 (ch / sh / th) ___ink	**2** (wr / ch / th) ___air	**3** (kn / wh / sh) ___ip
4 (th / wr / ch) ___umb	**5** (wh / wr / sh) ___eat	**6** (sh / kn / wr) ___ist
7 (sh / wh / th) ___eel	**8** (ch / wr / kn) ___ot	**9** (th / sh / wh) ___ell

Write a word from the box to complete each sentence.

child	know	share	Think	what	wrapped

10. _____ what it would be like to be a chair.

11. Does a chair _____ how useful it is?

12. A _____ can sit and read in a cozy chair.

13. Two friends can _____ a seat.

14. A child _____ in a blanket can go to sleep.

15. But _____ does a chair do when it is tired?

Clock ends with the consonant digraph **ck**. Each word in the box ends with a consonant digraph. Write the word that names each picture.

beach	brush	chick	clock	couch	dish
	fish	moth	peach	tooth	truck	wreath

1	2	3	4
_____	_____	_____	_____

5	6	7	8
_____	_____	_____	_____

9	10	11	12
_____	_____	_____	_____

 Work Together

Work with a partner. Write a word from above to complete each rhyme.

13. If I were a _____,
I'd tick and I'd tock.

14. If I were a _____,
I'd find a worm quick.

15. If I were a _____,
I'd swim and I'd swish.

16. If I were a _____,
I'd often say "Ouch!"

17. If I were a _____,
I'd eat holes in cloth.

18. If I were a _____,
I'd stay out of reach.

LESSON 36: Recognizing and Writing Final
Consonant Digraphs **ck, th, sh, ch**

 Ask your child to sort the words
in the box by final consonant
digraph: **ck, th, sh, ch**.

Name _____

Dishes has the consonant digraph **sh** in the middle. Circle the consonant digraph in each picture name. Then write the digraph to complete the word.

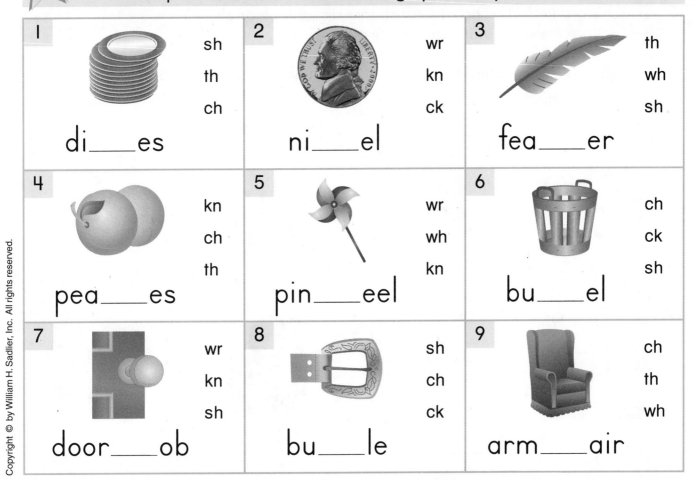

1	sh	2	wr	3	th
	th		kn		wh
	ch		ck		sh
di___es		ni___el		fea___er	

4	kn	5	wr	6	ch
	ch		wh		ck
	th		kn		sh
pea___es		pin___eel		bu___el	

7	wr	8	sh	9	ch
	kn		ch		th
	sh		ck		wh
door___ob		bu___le		arm___air	

Read the travel ad. Underline each word with a consonant digraph in the middle. Then circle the digraph.

Visit the enchanted Island of Friendship!

Sit awhile in the sunshine. Have fun splashing in the warm water.
Go somewhere interesting every day . . . or relax and do nothing.
Purchase a ticket quickly!
This trip makes a great birthday gift.

Imagine visiting the enchanted island. Write a postcard home.

Helpful Hint The consonant digraphs **ph** and **gh** can stand for the same sound.
phone   cou**gh**

Each word in the box has the consonant digraph **ph** or **gh**.
Write the word that names each picture.

| cough | dolphin | elephant | graph |
| laugh | phone | photo | trophy |

1	2	3	4
_____	_____	_____	_____

5	6	7	8
_____	_____	_____	_____

Circle each word with the consonant digraph **ph** or **gh**.
Then write **yes** or **no** to answer the question.

9. Can you make a phone call? _____

10. Does clean air make you cough? _____

11. Are most elephants tiny? _____

12. Do you laugh at funny jokes? _____

13. Can you hear a photo? _____

14. Can a dolphin draw a graph? _____

15. Is tree bark rough? _____

16. Is a trophy a prize? _____

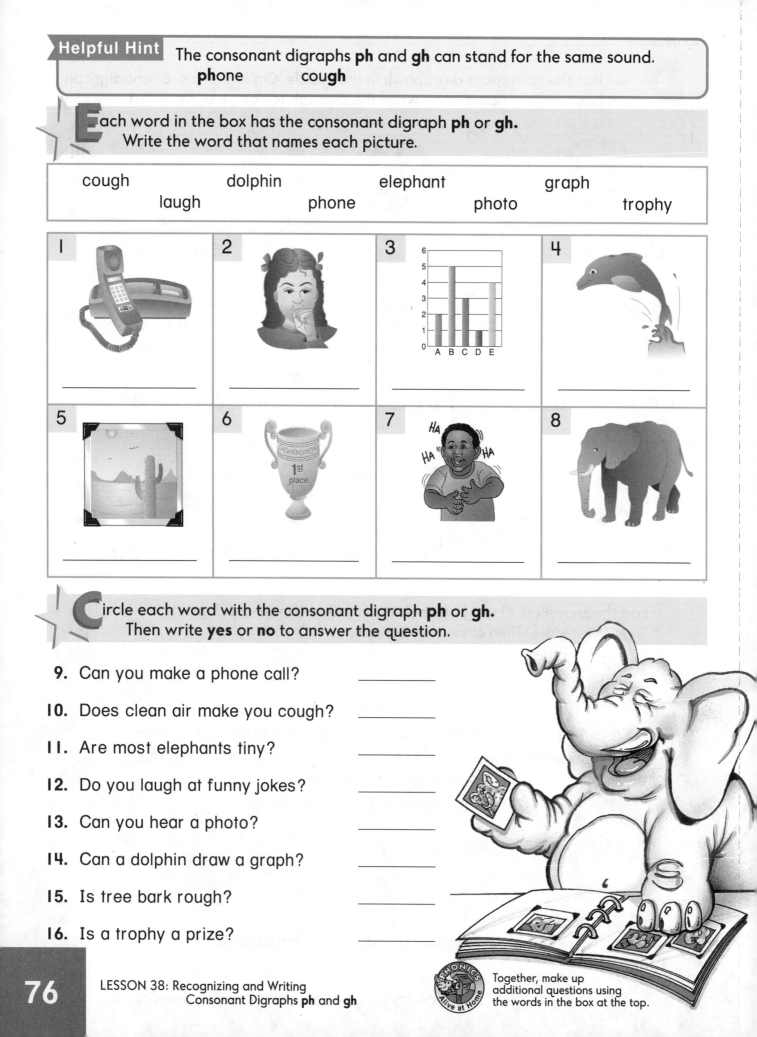

LESSON 38: Recognizing and Writing
Consonant Digraphs **ph** and **gh**

Together, make up
additional questions using
the words in the box at the top.

Name _____

You can use a syllable you know to help you read an unknown word.

chat   **chat**ter   **chat**ty

Say each syllable. Then combine the syllables to write a word.

1	chat + ter _____ chat + ty _____	**2**	sharp + en _____ sharp + er _____
3	thir + ty _____ thir + teen _____	**4**	wrap + per _____ wrap + ping _____
5	pho + to _____ pho + ny _____	**6**	teach + er _____ teach + es _____
7	quick + ly _____ quick + est _____	**8**	fish + ing _____ fish + y _____

Write the two-syllable word from above that fits each clue.
Then take turns reading the clues and answers with a partner.

9. It begins with **teach.**
It's someone who gives lessons.

The word is _____.

10. It begins with **pho.**
It's another word for **fake.**

The word is _____.

11. It begins with **fish.**
It describes how something smells.

The word is _____.

12. It begins with **sharp.**
It's what you do to a pencil.

The word is _____.

13. It begins with **quick.**
It's another word for **fastest.**

The word is _____.

14. It begins with **thir.**
It's one more than twelve.

The word is _____.

Rough Tough Phill

Rough Tough Phill was the biggest, strongest person in Wheelbarrow County. She could carry an elephant under her arm. She could ride a whale clear across the ocean and back. She could eat thirty bushels of peaches at one sitting.

One day Phill heard about The Strongest Person on Earth Contest. It was being held in Cherrytown, 7,629 miles away. Nothing would stop Phill from entering the contest and winning the trophy.

Phill set out for Cherrytown. She charged down the path like a herd of bulls. People heard thunder as Phill passed by. Boom! Crack! Crash! A huge rock turned to ashes when Phill stepped on it. A wild 645-foot snake slithered out.

1. Who was Rough Tough Phill?

_____

2. Why did she set out for Cherrytown?

_____

3. What do you think is the most amazing thing that Phill could do?

_____

_____

4. What do you think happens next in the story?

_____

_____

_____

_____

Ask your child to read "Rough Tough Phill" to you. Make up an ending for the story.

Name _____

Read the phrases in the box. Say and spell each word in bold print. Repeat the word. Then sort the words according to sound and spelling. One word can be listed under more than one heading.

the **crash** of thunder

turn a **doorknob**

a happy **laugh**

two for a **nickel**

nothing to do

phone home

shiny new pennies

somewhere over the rainbow

a **south** wind

warm **sunshine**

a **thick** fog

touch snowflakes

when it began to rain

wrapped in a blanket

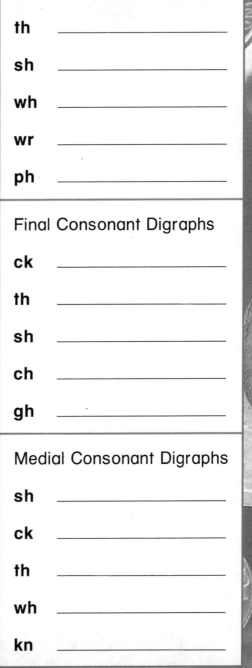

Initial Consonant Digraphs

th _____

sh _____

wh _____

wr _____

ph _____

Final Consonant Digraphs

ck _____

th _____

sh _____

ch _____

gh _____

Medial Consonant Digraphs

sh _____

ck _____

th _____

wh _____

kn _____

Spell, Write and Tell

Imagine that one day it rains sunflakes, pennies, or something else. Write a journal entry in which you describe the unusual weather and tell how you spent the day. In your entry, use one or more of your spelling words. Present your writing to classmates.

crash	doorknob	laugh	nickel	nothing	phone	shiny
somewhere	south	sunshine	thick	touch	when	wrapped

Date: _____

_____

_____

_____

_____

_____

_____

_____

_____

_____

_____

_____

LESSON 41: Connecting Spelling, Writing, and Speaking

Ask your child to act as a weather forecaster and to present his or her journal entry to you.

Name _____

Read the tall tale. Think about the problem that Lenny faces and how the problem is solved. Then answer the questions.

Lenny Longlegs and the Star

Lenny Longlegs was the tallest man who ever lived. He was so tall that he could see over trees, mountains, and buildings. When he walked, clouds tickled his nose. Sometimes this made him sneeze, which caused a tornado!

One night Lenny's friend Stella asked if he could touch the stars. Lenny said, "I'll try." He reached up with his enormous arm. He stretched and stretched, but not far enough.

"Jump," Stella suggested. Lenny jumped, but he still couldn't touch the twinkling stars.

"Jump from higher up," Stella said. "From a mountaintop."

Lenny climbed to the very top of the tallest mountain in the world. He took a deep breath and leaped as high as he could. His fingers curled around a star. Lenny pulled the star out of the sky and gave it to Stella.

1. What was Lenny's problem?

_____

_____

2. How did Lenny solve the problem?

_____

_____

Write your own tall tale. Introduce the smallest, smartest, fastest, or strongest person in the world. Tell about a problem he or she faces and solves. Use one or more words from the box.

Writer's Tips

- Start by telling what is special about your main character.
- Use details. Give examples of the amazing things the character can do.
- Tell about a problem that comes up. Have your character use his or her special abilities to solve the problem.

bridge

dragon

elephant

fly

nest

playground

rainbow

ship

sleep

swim

think

twist

_____

_____

_____

_____

_____

_____

_____

_____

_____

_____

_____

_____

_____

_____

_____

LESSON 42: Connecting Reading and Writing
Comprehension: Identifying Problem/Solution

Ask your child to read his or her tall tale to you. Together, make up another tall tale.

Name _____

Let's read and talk about rainbows.

The Golden Rainbow

What do you imagine when you see a rainbow in the sky? Long ago, people thought that following a rainbow's path would make them rich. They believed they would find a pot of gold at a rainbow's end.

Today we know a rainbow is not magical. It is simply a curve or bow made by sunlight shining on drops of water. Sunlight is made up of many colors. When the sunlight shines on raindrops, it divides into blue, green, yellow, orange, red, and other colors. The raindrops reflect the colors like a mirror. So, if the sun is behind you and rain is falling in front of you, you may see a rainbow in the sky.

The next time it rains, look for a rainbow. Notice where the sun is and where the rain is falling. Think about the reasons for rainbows.

How would you explain a rainbow to a friend?

LESSON 43: Syllables, Consonant Blends, Compound Words,
y as a Vowel, and Consonant Digraphs in Context
Comprehension: Understanding Cause and Effect

83

Write a consonant digraph to complete each picture name.

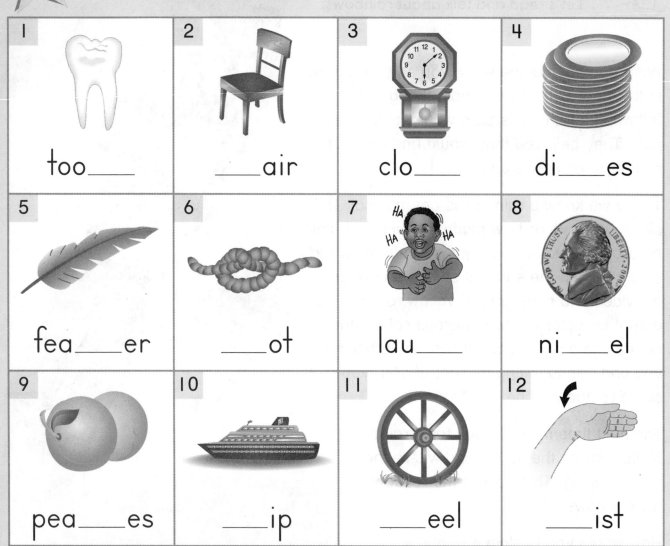

1 too___	2 ___air	3 clo___	4 di___es
5 fea___er	6 ___ot	7 lau___	8 ni___el
9 pea___es	10 ___ip	11 ___eel	12 ___ist

Fill in the circle next to the word that makes sense in each sentence.

13. Do you like to go to the ___? ○ leash ○ beach

14. What if you were a ___? ○ fish ○ quick

15. Do you ___ how you'd spend each day? ○ show ○ know

16. Would you like ___ in the sea? ○ splashing ○ packing

17. Would you go swimming with a ___? ○ dolphin ○ elephant

18. Or would you end up as somebody's ___? ○ dish ○ ship

19. I ___ I'd rather be me. ○ thing ○ think

84

Review this Check-Up with your child.

The Sidewalk Racer

Skimming
an asphalt sea
I swerve, I curve, I
sway; I speed to whirring
sound an inch above the
ground; I'm the sailor
and the sail; I'm the
driver and the wheel
I'm the one and only
single engine
human auto
mobile.

Lillian Morrison

Critical Thinking

Why does the sidewalk racer call herself a sailor and a sail,
a driver and a wheel, a single engine human automobile?

How else could you describe a sidewalk racer?

LESSON 44: **r**-controlled Vowels, Vowel Digraphs, and Diphthongs
Poetry: Rhythm

85

Phonics Alive at Home

Name _____

Dear Family,

In this unit about sports and games, your child will learn the sounds of vowel combinations. Share these definitions:

r-controlled vowel: an **r** after a vowel gives the vowel a new sound (st**ar**, t**or**ch, ch**air**, sp**ear**)

vowel digraph: two letters that come together to make a long, short, or special vowel sound (h**ea**d, s**ea**t, h**oo**k, b**oo**t)

diphthong: two letters blended together that can stand for one vowel sound (cl**ow**n, cl**ou**d, c**oi**ns, t**oy**s, cr**ew**)

• Read the poem on the reverse side. Talk about the way the sidewalk racer moves.

• Read the poem again. Ask your child to move like the sidewalk racer as you read.

• Search through the poem for words with **r**-controlled vowels, vowel digraphs, and diphthongs.

Apreciada Familia:

En esta unidad sobre los deportes los niños aprenderán los sonidos de vocales combinadas. Compartan las siguientes definiciones:

vocales controladas por la r: una **r** después de una vocal da a la vocal un nuevo sonido (st**ar**, t**or**ch, ch**air**, sp**ear**)

vocal dígrafa: dos letras que juntas hacen un sonido vocal largo, corto o especial (h**ea**d, s**ea**t, h**oo**k, b**oo**t)

diptongo: dos letras que juntas producen un solo sonido vocal (cl**ow**n, cl**ou**d, c**oi**ns, t**oy**s, cr**ew**)

• Lea el poema en la página 85. Hablen sobre la forma en que el corredor se mueve.

• Lea de nuevo el poema. Pida al niño moverse igual que el corredor mientras usted lee.

• Busquen palabras en el poema con vocales controladas por la **r**, vocales dígrafas, y diptongos.

PROJECT

Make a list of sidewalk games or sports, such as hopscotch, hoops, jump rope, and marbles. Circle any vowel combinations in the words on your list. Then play one of the games with your child.

PROYECTO

Hagan una lista de juegos o deportes que se pueden jugar en la acera como por ejemplo: canicas, rayuela, saltar la cuerda. Encierren en un círculo cualquier combinación de vocales en las palabras en su lista. Después jueguen uno de los juegos.

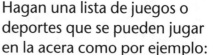

Helpful Hint   An **r** after a vowel gives the vowel a new sound.
st**ar**   t**or**ch   w**or**ld   ch**air**   sp**ear**

⭐ Circle and write the word that names each picture.

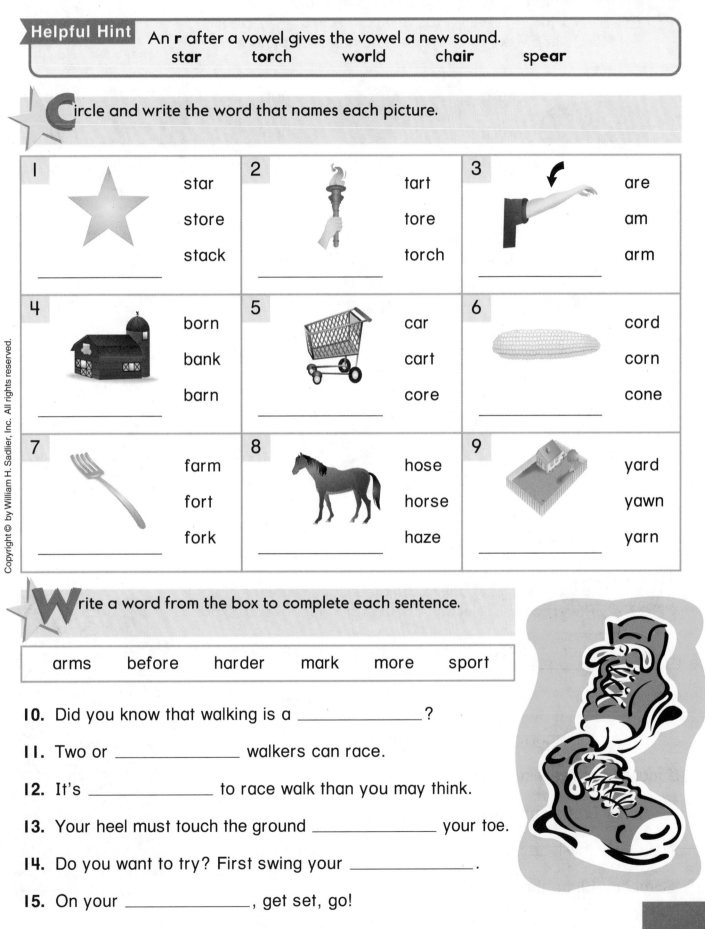

1	star store stack	2	tart tore torch	3	are am arm
_____		_____		_____	
4	born bank barn	5	car cart core	6	cord corn cone
_____		_____		_____	
7	farm fort fork	8	hose horse haze	9	yard yawn yarn
_____		_____		_____	

⭐ Write a word from the box to complete each sentence.

arms	before	harder	mark	more	sport

10. Did you know that walking is a _____?

11. Two or _____ walkers can race.

12. It's _____ to race walk than you may think.

13. Your heel must touch the ground _____ your toe.

14. Do you want to try? First swing your _____.

15. On your _____, get set, go!

Look at the different spellings for the same vowel sound.

w**or**ld   f**er**n   g**ir**l   c**ur**b   p**ear**l

Circle and write the word that names each picture.

1		2		3	
	word worth world _____		short sheet shirt _____		curb curl cub _____

4		5		6	
	pear pearl peas _____		farm fern for _____		girl grill gill _____

7		8		9	
	nurse north nose _____		work warm worm _____		pair perch per _____

Write a word from the box to complete each sentence.
Then read the selection about a girl who loves to skate.

bird	her	Pearl	third	turn	twirl	world

_____ is a young skater. She works hard at

_____ sport. She loves to jump and _____.

It makes her feel like a flying _____.

In her first competition, Pearl came in _____.

"Next year it will be my _____ to win," said Pearl.

"Someday I'll be the best in the _____."

LESSON 45: Recognizing and Writing Words
with or, er, ir, ur, ear

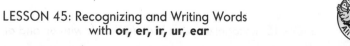

Ask your child to sort the words in the box at the bottom by spelling pattern: **or, er, ir, ur, ear.**

Name _____

Look at the different spellings for the same vowel sound.

ch**air**   squ**are**   p**ear**

Build words with this vowel sound. Add the initial letter or letters to each phonogram.

1	2	3
air	are	ear
ch _____	squ _____	p _____
f _____	d _____	w _____
h _____	sc _____	b _____
p _____	m _____	sw _____

Read the poem. Underline the words with **air, are,** or **ear.** Then write each word under the correct heading.

Rule number one is play fair.
Don't hog the ball—
Teammates share.
Never pull hair
Or act like a bear.
Don't scream and don't swear.
Show your teammates you care.

Words with **air**   Words with **are**   Words with **ear**

_____   _____   _____

_____   _____   _____

Write a sentence or two telling what fair play means to you.
Circle any words with **air, are,** or **ear.**

Look at the two spellings for the same vowel sound.

sp**ear**   d**eer**

Build words with this vowel sound. Add the initial letter or letters to each phonogram. Then write another word with the same phonogram. Make sure the **ear**-word you write has the same vowel sound.

1	2
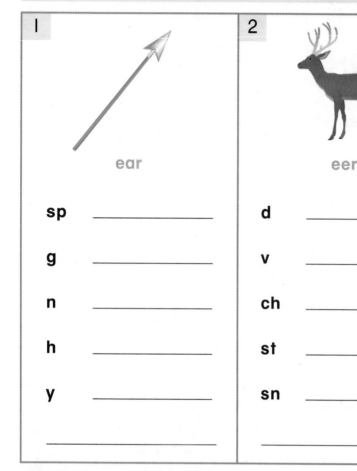 ear	eer
sp _____	d _____
g _____	v _____
n _____	ch _____
h _____	st _____
y _____	sn _____
_____	_____

Write a word from above to complete each sentence. Then take turns reading the sentences with a partner.

3. My neighborhood has a bike rodeo every _____.

4. Kids from _____ and far come to watch and to ride.

5. Each rider wears safety _____.

6. Good riders _____ clear of the orange cones.

7. Riders who _____ off course lose points.

8. We _____ for all the riders.

9. You can _____ us blocks away.

LESSON 46: Recognizing and Writing Words
with **ear** and **eer**

Together, write a two-line rhyme, using words with **ear** and **eer**.

Name _____

You can use a syllable you know to help you read an unknown word.

car   **car**bon   **car**go   **car**pet   **car**ton

Say the syllable at the beginning of each row. Circle the words that begin with the same syllable.

1	**gar**	garden	gerbil	garbage	gurgle
2	**per**	party	person	perfect	porridge
3	**cir**	circle	carton	corner	circus
4	**for**	furry	faraway	forget	forbid
5	**tur**	turtle	turkey	tornado	target
6	**mar**	merchant	market	marbles	murmur
7	**cur**	corner	cursive	carpet	current

Write a word from the box to complete each sentence. Use the syllable clues to help you.

carpet	order	party	perfect
tortoise	circle	person	cartoon

per   8. "Statues" is a _____ lawn game.

par   9. It's a good game for a _____.

or   10. You don't need to _____ special equipment.

car   11. Just play on a _____ of grass.

per   12. Ask one _____ to be the statue maker.

cir   13. He or she will swing you around in a _____ and tell you what to be.

car   14. Perhaps you can be a _____ or story character.

tor   15. Do you think you'd make a good _____ or hare?

LESSON 47: Syllables in Words with **r**-controlled Vowels

Draw a line from each syllable in the first column to a syllable in the second column to make a word. Write the word.

1

air   ful   <u>airport</u>

rare   cut   _____

cheer   port   _____

hair   ly   _____

2

arm   chair   _____

rein   ware   _____

a   pare   _____

pre   deer   _____

3

stair   y   _____

near   ring   _____

dair   by   _____

ear   way   _____

4

re   clear   _____

be   mare   _____

un   ware   _____

night   pair   _____

Work with a partner. Write the two-syllable word from above that fits each clue.

5. It begins with **cheer.**
It's another word for **happy.**

The word is _____.

6. It begins with **near.**
It means "close at hand."

The word is _____.

7. It begins with **dair.**
It's where milk and cream are kept.

The word is _____.

8. It ends with **clear.**
It describes bad directions.

The word is _____.

9. It ends with **ware.**
It means "watch out."

The word is _____.

10. It ends with **pair.**
It's another word for **fix.**

The word is _____.

11. It ends with **chair.**
It's a comfortable seat.

The word is _____.

12. It ends with **deer.**
It's an Arctic animal.

The word is _____.

With your child, write a riddle for each of the following words: **airport, earring, prepare, rarely.**

Name _____

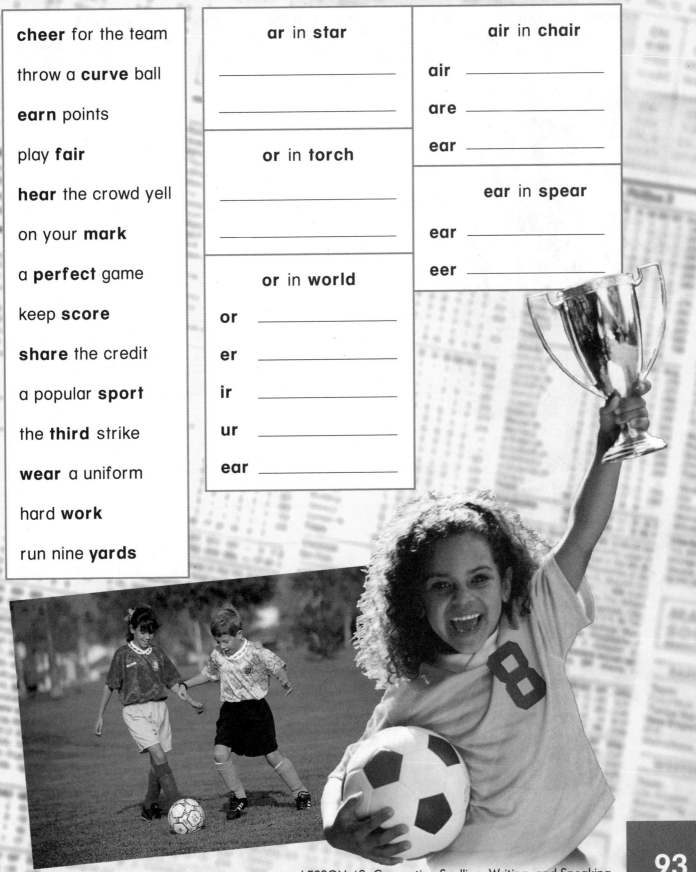

Spell Write, and Tell Read the phrases in the box. Say and spell each word in bold print. Repeat the word. Then sort the words according to sound and spelling.

cheer for the team

throw a **curve** ball

earn points

play **fair**

hear the crowd yell

on your **mark**

a **perfect** game

keep **score**

share the credit

a popular **sport**

the **third** strike

wear a uniform

hard **work**

run nine **yards**

ar in **star**

_____

_____

or in **torch**

_____

_____

or in **world**

or _____

er _____

ir _____

ur _____

ear _____

air in **chair**

air _____

are _____

ear _____

ear in **spear**

ear _____

eer _____

Spell Write and Tell

Be a sportswriter. Write an article about one of your favorite games or events. Begin with a lead sentence that tells **who, what, when,** and **where,** and use one or more of your spelling words. Publish the article for classmates to read.

cheer	curve	earn	fair	hear	mark	perfect
score	share	sport	third	wear	work	yards

headline →

by _____ ← byline

LESSON 48: Connecting Spelling, Writing, and Speaking

Together, read your child's article. Ask your child to point out the lead sentence.

Name _____

Write a word from the box for each clue. Then read down to find the answer to the question.

chair	deer	early	girl	herd	horse	near
nurse	pear	square	star	steer	word	worm

1. not a doctor, but a ___   ___ ___ ___ ___

2. apple, peach, or ___   ___ ___ ___ ___

3. ride a ___ or pony   ___ ___ ___ ___ ___

4. an antler of a ___   ___ ___ ___ ___

5. ___ a bike or car   ___ ___ ___ ___

6. not a circle, but a ___   ___ ___ ___ ___ ___ ___

7. an ___ bird   ___ ___ ___ ___ ___

8. not far, but ___   ___ ___ ___ ___

9. a ___ in a puzzle   ___ ___ ___ ___

10. not a boy, but a ___   ___ ___ ___ ___

11. throne, bench, or ___   ___ ___ ___ ___ ___

12. crawl like a ___   ___ ___ ___ ___

13. a ___ of cows   ___ ___ ___ ___

14. a ___ athlete   ___ ___ ___ ___

What is the theme of this unit?

_____

1 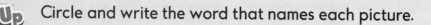 gear / girl / guard _____	**2** car / curl / corn _____	**3** per / purr / pear _____
4 world / word / worn _____	**5** born / barn / burn _____	**6** deer / door / dare _____
7 porch / pearl / perch _____	**8** spare / spear / spur _____	**9** chair / cheer / chore _____

Fill in the circle next to the word that fits each clue.

10. It's an animal with horns or what you do in a bike rodeo.
○ store   ○ steer   ○ stare

11. It's a carnival or a word that describes someone who is a good sport.
○ fair   ○ fear   ○ fern

12. It's a kind of baseball pitch or the shape of the letter **S**.
○ car   ○ curve   ○ care

13. It's a park in the center of town or the shape of a checkerboard.
○ squirt   ○ squirrel   ○ square

14. It's a very good player or what you see in the night sky.
○ star   ○ stair   ○ stir

15. It's an animal you can ride or something a gymnast jumps over.
○ hairs   ○ horse   ○ hers

 Review this Check-Up with your child.

Name _____

Helpful Hint A **vowel digraph** is two letters together that stand for one vowel sound. The vowel sound can be long or short, or the vowel digraph can have a sound of its own.

Listen for the different sounds of the vowel digraph **ea**.

head   s**ea**t

Say the words in the box. Write the short **e** words under the picture of the head. Write the long **e** words under the picture of the seat.

bread	each	eat	health		leaf
meals	spread	sweat		team	thread

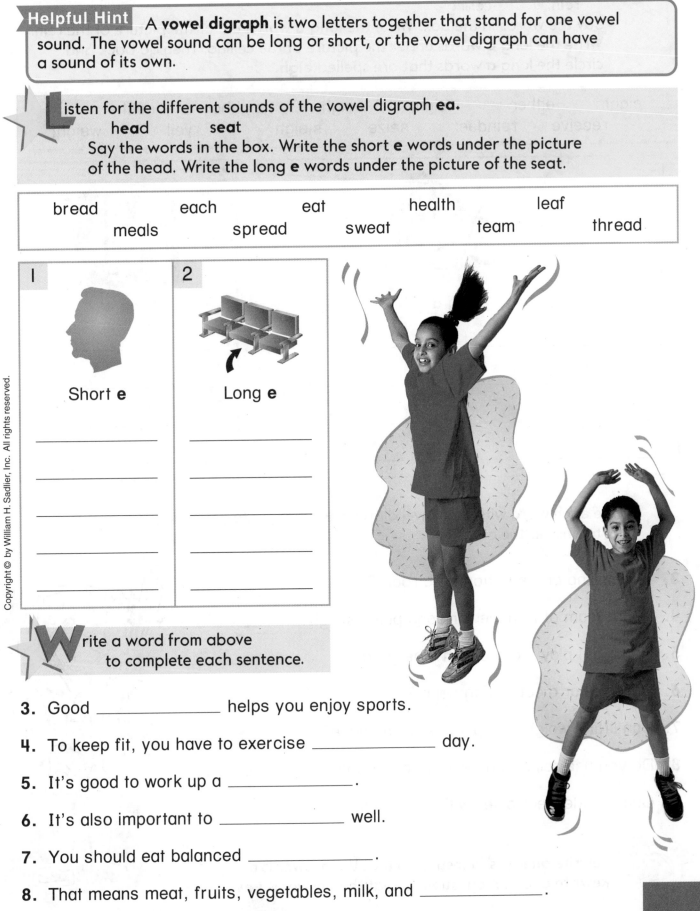

1	2
Short **e**	Long **e**
_____	_____
_____	_____
_____	_____
_____	_____
_____	_____

Write a word from above to complete each sentence.

3. Good _____ helps you enjoy sports.

4. To keep fit, you have to exercise _____ day.

5. It's good to work up a _____ .

6. It's also important to _____ well.

7. You should eat balanced _____ .

8. That means meat, fruits, vegetables, milk, and _____ .

Listen for the different sounds of the vowel digraph **ei.**

rein   ceiling

Say the words in the box. Write the long **a** words under the picture of the rein. Write the long **e** words under the picture of the ceiling. Then go back and circle the long **a** words that are spelled **eigh.**

eight	either	freight	neigh	neighbor	neither
receive	reindeer	seize	sleigh	veil	weight

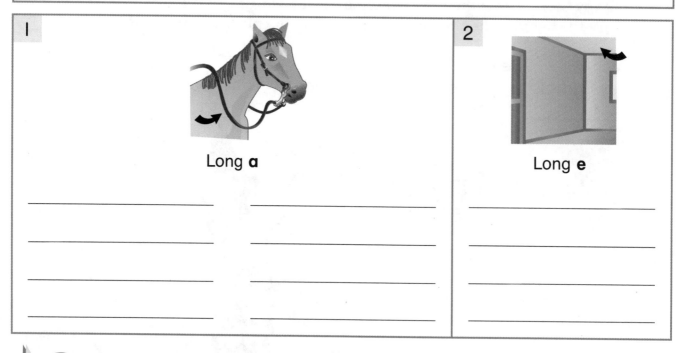

1

Long **a**

_____ _____

_____ _____

_____ _____

_____ _____

2

Long **e**

_____

_____

_____

_____

Circle each word with the vowel digraph **ei.** Then write **yes** or **no** to answer the question.

3. Is a ceiling at the bottom of a room? _____

4. Can a team of reindeer or dogs pull a sleigh? _____

5. Can a girl play a game with a neighbor? _____

6. Does either a cat or dog neigh? _____

7. Can lifting weights help you stay in shape? _____

8. Do you use reins to drive a freight train? _____

9. Can a bride wear a veil with her dress? _____

Rewrite one "yes" question so that the answer is **no.**
Rewrite one "no" question so that the answer is **yes.**

LESSON 51: Recognizing and Writing Vowel Digraph **ei**

With your child, take turns asking and answering the questions at the bottom of the page.

Name _____

Listen for the different sounds of the vowel digraph **oo.**

   h**oo**k   b**oo**t

The words in each box have the vowel digraph **oo.**
Write the word that fits each clue.

book	brook	foot	good
hook	stood	woods	wool

1. You use this to catch fish.   _____

2. This is a small stream.   _____

3. This is the opposite of **bad.**   _____

4. This is winter material.   _____

5. This is a place to set up camp.   _____

6. You can stand on this.   _____

7. This is a form of the word **stand.**   _____

8. You read this.   _____

boot	food	loose	noon
pool	smooth	soon	too

9. This is another word for **also.**   _____

10. You wear this on your foot.   _____

11. This is the opposite of **rough.**   _____

12. This is the opposite of **tight.**   _____

13. This is a place to go swimming.   _____

14. This means "in a short time."   _____

15. This is a time of day.   _____

16. You eat this.   _____

LESSON 52: Recognizing and Writing Vowel Digraph **oo**   **99**

The vowel digraphs **au, aw,** and **al** have the same vowel sound.

la**u**nch   str**aw**   b**al**l

Each word in the box has this vowel sound. Write the word that names each picture.

August	ball	chalk	crawl	faucet	hawk
launch	salt	straw	vault	wall	yawn

1. _____

2. _____

3. _____

4. _____

5. _____

6. _____

7. _____

8. _____

9. _____

10. _____

11. _____

12. _____

Circle and write the word that completes each sentence.

13. Baseball usually makes me _____ . yawn dawn

14. But the last game in _____ was really exciting. awning August

15. The first two batters _____ . launched walked

16. The next batter watched the ball like a _____ . hawk haul

17. Then he hit it toward the left _____ . wall call

18. I _____ it sail into the stands. raw saw

19. Guess who caught the _____ ! ball straw

LESSON 53: Recognizing and Writing Vowel
Digraphs **au, aw, al**

Ask your child to use in a sentence each answer choice that is not circled in items 13–19.

Name _____

You can use a syllable you know to help you read an unknown word.
    head   **read**y   in**stead**

Write the one-syllable word that you can use to help you read each two-syllable word.

1	hawk	head	pea	weigh

ready   _____

neighbor   _____

awkward   _____

eager   _____

2	call	freight	too	bread

instead   _____

lightweight _____

igloo   _____

softball   _____

3	all	beak	book	vein

rookie   _____

also   _____

weaken   _____

reindeer   _____

4	ball	sweat	seal	soon

oatmeal   _____

cartoon   _____

sweater   _____

snowfall   _____

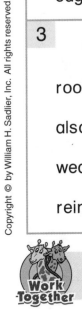

Write a two-syllable word from above to answer each question. Compare answers with a partner.

5. What word with the digraph **ei** names an Arctic animal? _____

6. What word with the digraph **ea** names something you wear? _____

7. What word with the digraph **aw** is the opposite of **graceful**? _____

8. What word with the digraph **oo** is a first-year player? _____

9. What word with the digraph **ea** names a cereal? _____

10. What word with the digraph **oo** is a funny drawing? _____

11. What word with the digraph **al** names a summer sport? _____

You can use a syllable you know to help you read an unknown word.

head   a**head**

R ead each riddle. Look at the syllables in the words in bold print and write the two-syllable word that fits the clue.

1. It starts like **around.**
   It ends like **forehead.**
   It means "in front."

   The word is _____.

2. It starts like **seaweed.**
   It ends like **poison.**
   It's a time of the year.

   The word is _____.

3. It starts like **toothbrush.**
   It ends like **weightless.**
   It describes a baby.

   The word is _____.

4. It starts like **mushy.**
   It ends like **classroom.**
   It's also a toadstool.

   The word is _____.

5. It starts like **repeat.**
   It ends like **deceive.**
   It means "to get."

   The word is _____.

6. It starts like **walnut.**
   It ends like **virus.**
   It's an animal with tusks.

   The word is _____.

7. It starts like **footprint.**
   It ends like **baseball.**
   It's a fall sport.

   The word is _____.

8. It starts like **autumn.**
   It ends like **photo.**
   It's another word for **car.**

   The word is _____.

Write On

Work with a classmate to write a riddle for a two-syllable word. Challenge a friend to solve it.

LESSON 54: Syllables in Words with Vowel Digraphs

Name _____

Spell, Write and Tell

Read the phrases in the box. Say and spell each word in bold print. Repeat the word. Then sort the words according to sound and spelling.

caught the ball

eager to play

at **either** end

not my **fault**

a **good** game

get **ready**

smooth sailing

be over **soon**

work up a **sweat**

make the **team**

walk to first base

lift **weights**

into the **woods**

makes me **yawn**

ea in **head**	**ea** in **seat**
_____	_____
_____	_____

eigh in **eight**	**ei** in **ceiling**
_____	_____

oo in **hook** or **boot**	**au** in **launch**
_____	au _____
_____	aw _____
_____	al _____
_____	augh _____

Spell, Write, and Tell

Imagine what it's like to be a bat, a ball, or even a bench at a ball game. Write a paragraph telling how you feel. Be sure to use the word **I** and one or more of your spelling words. Share the paragraph with the class.

caught	eager	either	fault	good	ready	smooth
soon	sweat	team	walk	weights	woods	yawn

LESSON 55: Connecting Spelling, Writing, and Speaking

Ask your child to read his or her paragraph to you and to point out words with vowel combinations.

Name _____

Read the selection about a Chinese game.
Then answer the questions.

In China dragons mean good luck. So dragons are part of each New Year's celebration. You can join the fun by playing a game called 1-2-3 Dragon. Here is how to play.

Line up with at least eight other children. Put your hands on the shoulders of the person ahead of you. The very first person becomes the Dragon's Head. The last person becomes the Dragon's Tail.

The Tail starts the game by screaming "1-2-3 Dragon!" Then the Dragon starts to run. The Head leads the way, and the others hold on. The Head tries to seize and tag the Tail without breaking the Dragon.

This is not as easy as it sounds. Holding on makes moving awkward. As the Dragon twists and turns, the line gets crooked. If it falls apart, the Dragon is dead. The Head moves to the end of the line and becomes the Tail. A new Head tries to catch the Dragon's Tail.

1. What is the object of the game 1-2-3 Dragon?

_____

_____

2. What happens when the Dragon "breaks"?

_____

_____

3. How do you think points are scored in this game?

_____

_____

**Say the word at the beginning of each row.
Circle the words that have the same vowel sound.**

1	**ball**	ahead	also	straw	wool
2	**head**	weaken	smooth	thread	bread
3	**hook**	hawk	book	oatmeal	woods
4	**rein**	sleigh	walrus	freight	either
5	**launch**	salt	yawn	leaf	mushroom
6	**seat**	health	weight	seize	season
7	**boot**	vault	noon	too	chalk
8	**ceiling**	receive	reins	team	ready

Fill in the circle next to the word that makes sense in each sentence.

9. It's fun to go skating with your ____.
   ○ neighbors   ○ either   ○ neither

10. Use your ____ and you'll have a good time.
    ○ health   ○ hood   ○ head

11. Make sure your skates are neither ____ nor tight.
    ○ loom   ○ loose   ○ lease

12. Wear a helmet in case you ____.
    ○ fool   ○ crawl   ○ fall

13. ____ wear elbow, knee, and wrist pads.
    ○ Autumn   ○ August   ○ Also

14. Don't worry if your ankles are ____ at first.
    ○ walk   ○ weak   ○ wool

15. Just practice! ____ you'll do fine.
    ○ Soon   ○ Seat   ○ Saw

Review this Check-Up
with your child.

Name _____

Ads usually mix fact and opinion. A fact is true. It can be proved. An opinion cannot be proved. Read the ad. Think about which sentences state facts and which give opinions. Then answer the questions.

NEW Zappos Sneakers!

Finally, they're here! They're the latest and greatest! The perfect sneakers! New **Zappos**!

Zappos are the most comfortable sneakers you'll ever wear! They are made of soft, smooth leather. They have special padding in the heels. They have extra space for your toes.

What's more, **Zappos** are the best-looking sneakers in the world! They come in five different styles and colors. Choose from Sparkle Red, Marble Blue, Turtle Green, Torch Yellow, and Pearl White.

And here's another great thing. All this month, you'll receive a free **Zappos** shirt with each pair that you purchase.

So run, don't walk, to your nearest store. Get yourself **Zappos**!

I. What facts about Zappos sneakers are stated in the ad? List two.

_____

_____

2. What opinions about Zappos sneakers are given in the ad?

_____

_____

LESSON 57: Connecting Reading and Writing
Comprehension: Distinguishing Fact/Opinion

107

Read and **Write**

Imagine that you have a pair of Zappos. Are they as good as the ad claims? Write a letter to the Zappos Company. Tell why you like or dislike the sneakers—and the ad. Use one or more words from the box.

Writer's Tips

- Use the business letter form.
- Introduce yourself and tell why you are writing the letter.
- Give facts and details to support your opinion.
- Be polite.

heading → _____

_____

_____

Customer Service
Zappos Sneakers   ← inside address
400 High Street
Shoetown, USA 10001

Dear Sir or Madam,   ← greeting

body →

_____

_____

_____

_____

_____

_____

_____

_____

_____

closing → _____

signature → _____

care
comfortable
each
foot
neighborhood
perfect
return
softball
sports
too
wear
worst

108

LESSON 57: Connecting Reading and Writing
Comprehension: Distinguishing Fact/Opinion

Ask your child to read his or her letter to you. Together, write a letter from Zappos in response.

Helpful Hint A **diphthong** is two letters blended together that can stand for one vowel sound.

The diphthongs **ow** and **ou** have the same vowel sound.
cl**ow**n   cl**ou**d
Circle and write the word that names each picture.

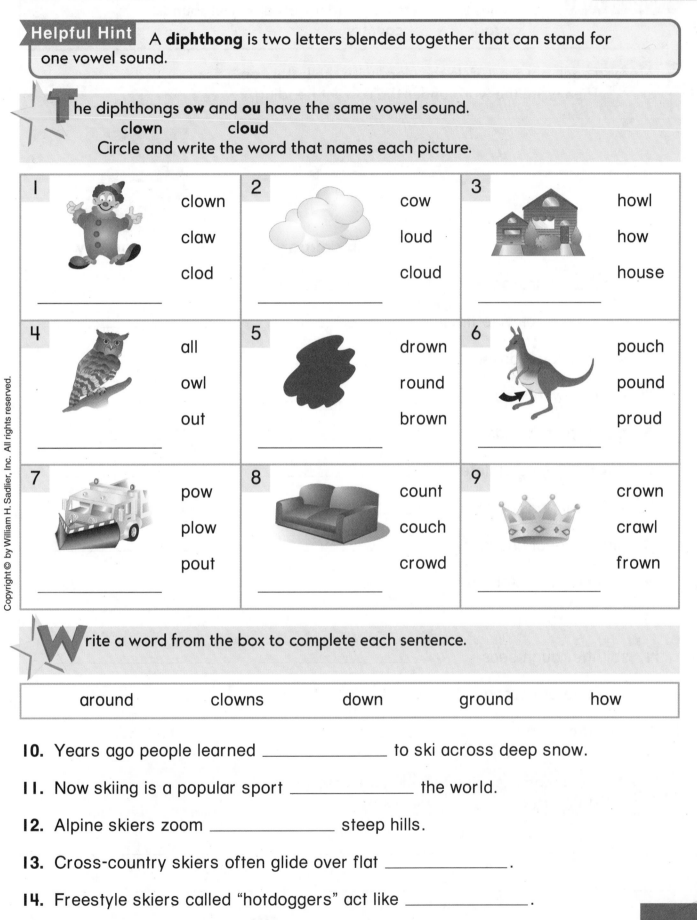

1.
clown
claw
clod
_____

2.
cow
loud
cloud
_____

3.
howl
how
house
_____

4.
all
owl
out
_____

5.
drown
round
brown
_____

6.
pouch
pound
proud
_____

7.
pow
plow
pout
_____

8.
count
couch
crowd
_____

9.
crown
crawl
frown
_____

Write a word from the box to complete each sentence.

around	clowns	down	ground	how

10. Years ago people learned _____ to ski across deep snow.

11. Now skiing is a popular sport _____ the world.

12. Alpine skiers zoom _____ steep hills.

13. Cross-country skiers often glide over flat _____.

14. Freestyle skiers called "hotdoggers" act like _____.

Read each phrase. Circle the word with the letters **ou.**
Then write the word under the correct heading.

ou in **cougar**   **ou** in **country**

1. good to hear from you _____ _____

2. a couple of bicycle tires _____ _____

3. score a touchdown _____ _____

4. sip a bowl of soup _____ _____

5. a group of friends _____ _____

6. several young athletes _____ _____

7. save coupons _____ _____

8. play a double header _____ _____

9. enough seats for all _____ _____

10. follow a routine _____ _____

11. sail the rough seas _____ _____

12. a troupe of acrobats _____ _____

13. a first cousin _____ _____

Write a sentence using two or more words with **ou.**
Read your sentence to a partner.

_____

_____

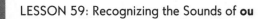 Ask your child to read the words
in one list to you. Read the words
in the other list to your child.

Name _____

The diphthongs **oi** in **coins** and **oy** in **toys** have the same vowel sound.
The diphthong **ew** has the vowel sound in **screw.**

coins   toys   screw

Say the words in the box. Then sort the words according to vowel sound.
Write each word under the correct heading.

annoy	boil	drew	flew	join	joy
knew	loyal	new	noise	spoil	toys

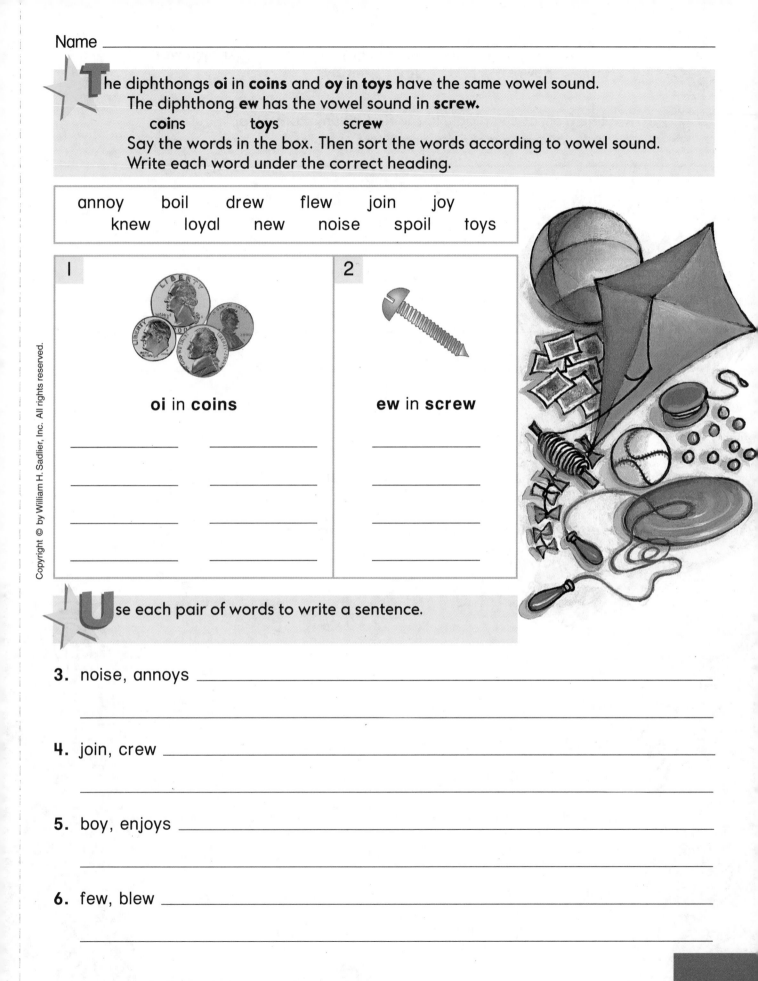

1

oi in **coins**

_____   _____

_____   _____

_____   _____

_____   _____

2

ew in **screw**

_____

_____

_____

_____

Use each pair of words to write a sentence.

3. noise, annoys _____

_____

4. join, crew _____

_____

5. boy, enjoys _____

_____

6. few, blew _____

_____

You can use a syllable you know to help you read an unknown word.

pow   power   joy   enjoy

Draw a line from each syllable in the first column to a syllable in the second column to make a word. Write the word.

1

pow	how	power
eye	er	_____
some	down	_____
touch	brow	_____

2

out	round	_____
play	doors	_____
a	ground	_____
cloud	y	_____

3

spoil	ing	_____
en	y	_____
nois	al	_____
loy	joy	_____

4

few	new	_____
re	few	_____
neph	er	_____
cur	ew	_____

Complete each line of the poem by writing a two-syllable word from above. Use the syllable clues to help you.

Let's Hear It for Fans!

loy   Our team has very _____ fans.

nois   They're really _____ in the stands.

cloud   And even on a _____ day,

out   They'll come _____ to watch us play.

round   The fans _____ us cheer out loud,

new   _____ our spirits, make us proud.

pow   It's their cheers that give us _____.

Let's name our fans "Fans of the Hour."

LESSON 61: Syllables in Words with Diphthongs

Ask your child to explain how he or she completed the poem. Then take turns reading pairs of lines.

Name _____

Spell, Write, and Tell

Read the phrases in the box. Say and spell each word in bold print. Repeat the word. Then sort the words according to sound and spelling.

act like **clowns**

collect **coins**

join the **crew**

a large **crowd**

enjoy the game

make **fewer** moves

flew a kite

in the **house**

a **loyal** teammate

too much **noise**

the third **out**

make us **proud**

spoil the fun

threw the ball

ou in cloud

ow _____

_____

ou _____

_____

_____

oy in toys

oi _____

_____

_____

oy _____

_____

ew in screw

_____

_____

_____

_____

Spell, Write, and Tell

Cheer on your favorite team! First use a spelling word to complete the cheer below. Then write two cheers of your own, using one or more spelling words. Lead the class in one of the cheers.

clowns	coins	crew	crowd	enjoy	fewer	flew
house	loyal	noise	out	proud	spoil	threw

Stamp your feet!
Cheer and shout!
Watch our pitchers

Strike them _____!

_____

_____

_____

_____

_____

_____

_____

_____

_____

_____

_____

_____

LESSON 62: Connecting Spelling, Writing, and Speaking

Ask your child to lead you in a cheer. Then write a cheer together. Use one or more spelling words.

Name _____

Complete the puzzle. Write a word from the box for each clue.

annoy   cloudy   crew   crowd   down   enjoy   eyebrow   fewer
flew   join   loyal   noise   outdoors   outs   owl

ACROSS ➡

1. less than a few

3. covered with clouds

4. be happy with

7. the opposite of **indoors**

8. pester

10. a large group of people

12. more than one out

13. a wise bird

DOWN ⬇

1. a form of the word **fly**

2. hair above the eye

5. put together

6. faithful

9. another word for **sound**

10. the sailors on a ship

11. the opposite of **up**

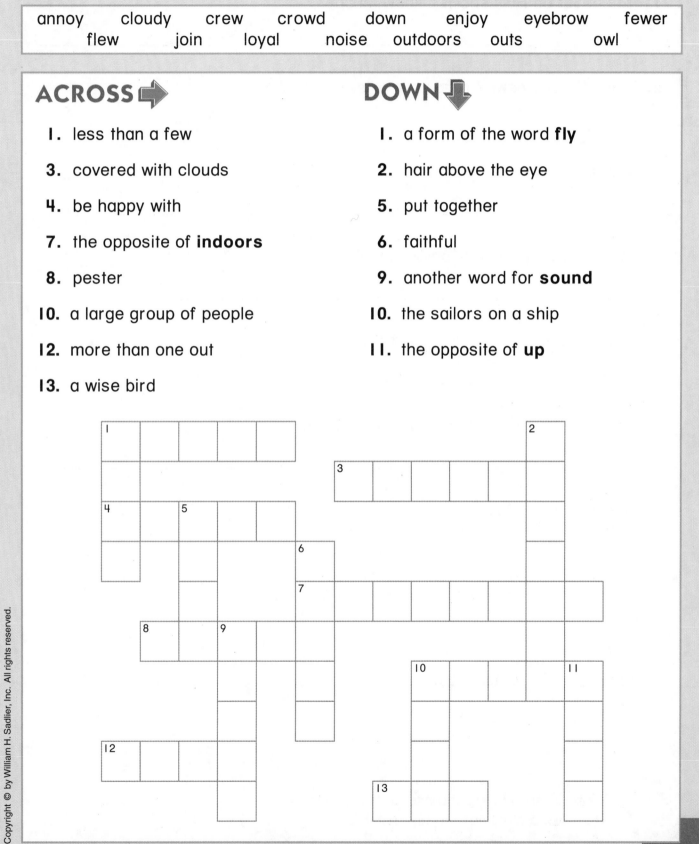

Unscramble each set of words to write a sentence that makes sense.

1. you about do How sports? know much

   _____

2. enjoy Do you news? reading sports

   _____

3. soccer. fans loyal watch Crowds of

   _____

4. team sports. play Girls boys and often

   _____

5. women or Men crew. join can a sailing

   _____

6. take part Cowhands in rodeos. clowns and

   _____

7. baseball outs. One inning six has

   _____

8. bounce you In basketball, the ball you move. as

   _____

9. spoil shot. Loud noise a can golfer's

   _____

Write a scrambled sentence about sports.
Then ask a classmate to unscramble it.

116

Ask your child to go back and to
say and circle one word with each
diphthong: **ow, ou, oi, oy, ew.**

Name _____

Read the article about a famous race. Pay attention to details. Then answer the questions.

Race Across Alaska

It's a race like no other. It's famous around the world. And it's probably the toughest race there is. It's called the Iditarod, and it's held every year in Alaska.

In this amazing race, teams of dogs pull sleds across more than 1,000 miles of ice, deep snow, and rough woods. Each team has between 12 and 18 dogs. Each sled has a driver, called a "musher."

About 75 teams begin the race, which takes from two to three weeks. But not all reach the finish line. The frozen ground is rough, uneven, and often steep. Temperatures go down far below zero. The howling wind whips snow around so that drivers and dogs cannot see.

Still, mushers and dogs come back year after year because they enjoy the challenge. "If you finish at all," says one racer, "you feel like you've won."

1. How many dogs are on each sled team?

_____

_____

2. Give two reasons why many teams do not reach the finish line.

_____

_____

LESSON 64: Connecting Reading and Writing
Comprehension: Recalling Details

Would you like to race in the Iditarod? Why or why not? Write a paragraph in which you tell your feelings about taking part in this challenging event. Use one or more words from the box.

Writer's Tips

- Begin with a topic sentence that tells whether or not you would like to take part in the race.

- Give at least two reasons why you feel the way you do. Use details from the article to help explain your feelings.

before

breath

down

enjoy

few

harder

join

powerful

rough

scare

stood

young

Ask your child to read his or her paragraph to you. Discuss your feelings about the Iditarod with your child.

Look and Learn

Let's read and talk about jumping rope.

If you have ever jumped rope with your friends, you know jumping rope is good exercise and fun, too. But is it a sport? Think about Double Dutch jump teams.

In Double Dutch, pairs of twirlers turn two ropes at once in opposite directions. The jumpers either dance or tumble as they jump. Performing on a jump team takes strength, energy, coordination, and teamwork.

Boys and girls who join jump teams all work very hard. They carefully prepare and practice new tricks with their team. When jumpers are ready, they enter contests and appear in shows.

Would you call jumping rope a sport? Why or why not?

LESSON 65: **r**-controlled Vowels, Vowel Digraphs, and Diphthongs in Context
Comprehension: Making Judgments

Say the word at the beginning of each row.
Circle the words that have the same vowel sound.

1	**clown**	clean	owl	foul	draw
2	**toys**	coins	boy	group	couch
3	**screw**	few	screen	new	now
4	**join**	bone	boil	jail	joy
5	**cloud**	fold	pouch	ground	claw
6	**threw**	blew	three	thaw	drew
7	**crowd**	crawl	crown	news	plow
8	**spoil**	noise	split	loyal	trail

Fill in the circle next to the word that makes sense in each sentence.

9. When the wind blows hard, surfers go ____ to the beach.
   ○ down   ○ dawn   ○ dew

10. These are people who ____ riding the waves.
   ○ joy   ○ enjoy   ○ annoy

11. The ____ roar of the ocean is music to their ears.
   ○ lead   ○ loud   ○ load

12. Some surf with speed and with ____.
   ○ powder   ○ tower   ○ power

13. A ____ will even beat the wind.
   ○ flew   ○ few   ○ foul

14. They all know that surfboards and sailboards are not ____.
   ○ toys   ○ toes   ○ tows

15. Only the best swimmers ____ in on this sport.
   ○ spoil   ○ coin   ○ join

Review this Check-Up
with your child.

I Made a Mechanical Dragon

I made a mechanical dragon
Of bottle tops, hinges, and strings,
Of thrown-away clocks and unmendable socks,
Of hangers and worn innersprings.
I built it of cardboard and plastic,
Of doorknobs and cables and corks,
Of spools and balloons and unusable spoons,
And rusty old hinges and forks.

It's quite an unusual dragon
It rolls on irregular wheels,
It clatters and creaks and it rattles and squeaks,
And when it tips over, it squeals.
I've tried to control its maneuvers,
It fails to obey my commands,
It bumps into walls till it totters and falls—
I made it myself with my hands!

Jack Prelutsky

Critical Thinking

What materials would you use to make a mechanical dragon?

What wonderful thing would you like to invent? How would you go about it?

Visit us at
www.sadlier-oxford.com

Name _____

Dear Family,

As your child progresses through this unit about inventions, she or he will learn about contractions and word endings. Share these definitions:

contraction: two words written as one with one or more letters left out (**didn't** = **did not; she'll** = **she will**)

plural: word that means more than one (**pencils, boxes, leaves**)

possessive: word that shows something belongs to someone (**the girl's bike; ten girls' bikes**)

word endings s, es, ing, and ed: endings that can be added to a word to make new words (**paints, fixes, running, smiled**)

• Read the poem on the reverse side. Invite your child to clap out the rhythm as you read.

• Take turns finding rhyming words, such as **strings** and **springs,** in the poem. Also look for contractions, plurals, and words that end in **s** or **ed.**

Apreciada Familia:

A medida que los niños progresan en esta unidad acerca de los inventos, aprenderán contracciones y terminaciones. Compartan estas definiciones:

contracción: una palabra formada por la abreviación de dos palabras (**didn't** = **did not; she'll** = **she will**)

plural: palabras que indican más de uno (**pencils, boxes, leaves**)

posesivo: palabras que indican que una cosa pertenece a alguien (**the girl's bike; ten girls' bikes**)

palabras que terminan en s, es, ing, y ed: letras que se añaden al final de una palabra para formar una nueva (**paints, fixes, running, smiled**)

• Lea el poema en la página 121. Invite al niño a aplaudir rítmicamente mientras usted lee.

• Túrnence para buscar en el poema palabras que rimen como por ejemplo: **strings** y **springs.** También busquen contracciones, plurales y palabras que terminen en **s** o en **ed.**

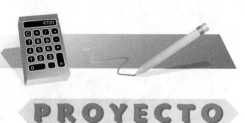

PROJECT

Help your child write and illustrate a story about life without paper, pencils, or some other invention. Circle contractions and word endings in the story.

PROYECTO

Ayude al niño a escribir e ilustrar un cuento sobre la vida sin papel, lápices o otro invento. Encierren en un círculo las contracciones y palabras con terminaciones.

122 LESSON 66: Syllables, Contractions, and Word Endings—Phonics Alive at Home

Name _____

Helpful Hint Every **syllable** has a vowel sound. Words can have one or more syllables.
umbrella—**3** vowel sounds—**3** syllables

Empty the junk box. Say the name of each thing you find and listen for the number of vowel sounds. Write each word under the correct heading. Then add a word of your own to each category.

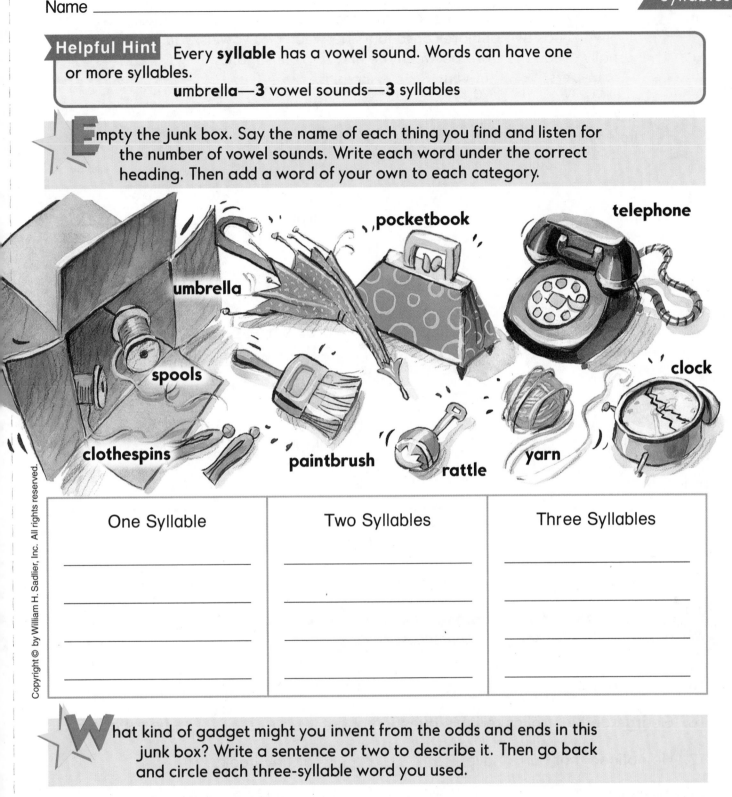

One Syllable	Two Syllables	Three Syllables
_____	_____	_____
_____	_____	_____
_____	_____	_____
_____	_____	_____

What kind of gadget might you invent from the odds and ends in this junk box? Write a sentence or two to describe it. Then go back and circle each three-syllable word you used.

_____

_____

_____

LESSON 67: Recognizing Syllables in Multisyllabic Words

123

One way to figure out an unknown word is to divide it into syllables. If a word has two or more consonants between two vowels, you can usually divide the word between the first two consonants.

zip-pers   **in-ve**nt   **sur-pri**se
VC CV   VC CV   VC CCV

Write each word, dividing it into syllables with a hyphen.

1 zippers _____	2 surprise _____
3 number _____	4 pencil _____
5 invent _____	6 problem _____
7 silver _____	8 wonder _____
9 hundreds _____	10 pilgrim _____
11 attach _____	12 fifty _____
13 fabric _____	14 tennis _____

Write a word from above to complete each sentence.
Take turns reading the sentences with a partner.

15. Did you ever _____ why burrs stick to clothes?

16. George de Mestral asked this question about _____ years ago.

17. He noticed that burrs have _____ of tiny hooks.

18. The hooks _____ themselves to thread loops on clothes.

19. Mr. de Mestral set out to _____ a fastener that would work like a burr.

20. His invention has replaced many _____ and buttons.

Ask your child to use items 1–14 to explain what a VCCV word is.

Name _____

If a word has one consonant between two vowels, first divide before the consonant. The first vowel sound will usually be long. If you still don't recognize the word, divide after the consonant. The vowel sound will usually be short.

o-ver   **mu-sic**   **pat-ent**   **clev-er**
V CV   V CV   VC V   VC V

⭐ **W**rite each word, dividing it into syllables with a hyphen.

1 over	_____	2 patent	_____
3 figure	_____	4 cozy	_____
5 never	_____	6 music	_____
7 clever	_____	8 frozen	_____
9 level	_____	10 value	_____

⭐ **W**rite a word from above to complete each sentence. Then read the paragraph about a clever young inventor.

As a young boy, Chester Greenwood liked to skate on a

_____ pond near his home. He dressed warmly,

but he could _____ keep his ears warm. Chester

spent hours trying to _____ out a way to solve his

problem. Finally he twisted some wire to fit _____

his head. His grandmother sewed fur on at the ear _____.

With his new earmuffs, Chester felt _____

and warm. Chester knew the _____ of his invention

and got a _____ for it. What a _____ boy!

Write each word, dividing it into syllables with a hyphen. Use the word strategy for VCV words to help you.

1. dragon _____	2. ever _____
3. pilot _____	4. river _____
5. finish _____	6. famous _____
7. seconds _____	8. palace _____
9. travel _____	10. lazy _____
11. tiger _____	12. magic _____
13. model _____	14. robot _____

Work with a partner. Use each pair of words to write a sentence.

15. famous, pilot _____

_____

16. model, robot _____

_____

17. magic, dragon _____

_____

18. ever, travel _____

_____

19. finish, seconds _____

_____

Ask your child to use the words at the top to explain what a VCV word is.

Name _____

Helpful Hint Some words end in a consonant followed by **le**. The **le** and the consonant before it often form a syllable.

puz-**zle**   ta-**ble**

Circle the syllable that completes each picture name. Then write the letters to complete the word.

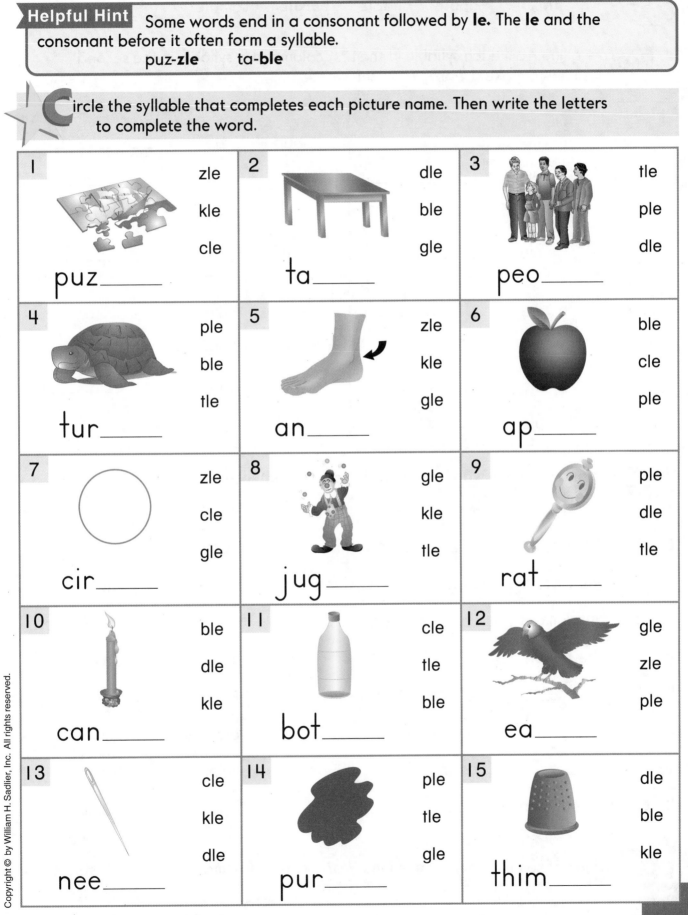

1	zle / kle / cle	puz_____
2	dle / ble / gle	ta_____
3	tle / ple / dle	peo_____
4	ple / ble / tle	tur_____
5	zle / kle / gle	an_____
6	ble / cle / ple	ap_____
7	zle / cle / gle	cir_____
8	gle / kle / tle	jug_____
9	ple / dle / tle	rat_____
10	ble / dle / kle	can_____
11	cle / tle / ble	bot_____
12	gle / zle / ple	ea_____
13	cle / kle / dle	nee_____
14	ple / tle / gle	pur_____
15	dle / ble / kle	thim_____

You can use a syllable you know to help you read an unknown word.

ple   a**pple**   ma**ple**   pur**ple**   sam**ple**

Draw a line from each syllable in the first column to a syllable in the second column to make a word. Write the word.

1

ap	tle	apple
han	dle	_____
bu	ple	_____
gen	gle	_____

2

bub	zle	_____
un	fle	_____
siz	cle	_____
ruf	ble	_____

3

noo	dle	_____
spar	kle	_____
rip	ble	_____
sta	ple	_____

4

ea	dle	_____
tur	ble	_____
a	tle	_____
sad	gle	_____

Circle and write the word that completes each sentence.

5. This is a very _____ invention.   sample   simple

6. It comes from the _____ East.   Middle   Muddle

7. It is round like a _____.   uncle   circle

8. It can be big or _____.   little   able

9. _____ have many uses for it.   Purple   People

10. A _____ has two of it.   bicycle   icicle

11. A _____ has three of it.   twinkle   tricycle

12. Can you solve the _____?   ripple   riddle

Think of some uses for the wheel. Work with a classmate to make a list.

Together, make up sentences using the words in the boxes at the top.

Name _____

Helpful Hint The vowels **a, i, o, u,** and **e** can stand for the same sound in an unstressed syllable. This sound is called the **schwa** sound.

sal′**a**d   rob′**i**n   lem′**o**n   cir′**cus**   sev′**e**n

Put the syllables together to name each picture. Circle the syllable with the schwa sound. Write the vowel that stands for the sound.

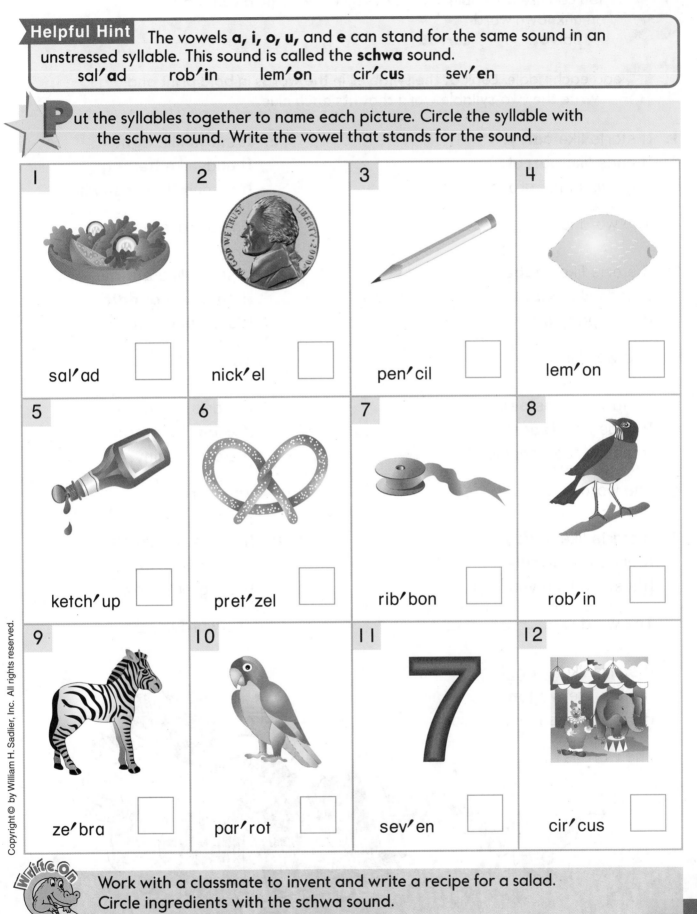

1 sal′ad	2 nick′el	3 pen′cil	4 lem′on
5 ketch′up	6 pret′zel	7 rib′bon	8 rob′in
9 ze′bra	10 par′rot	11 sev′en	12 cir′cus

Work with a classmate to invent and write a recipe for a salad. Circle ingredients with the schwa sound.

You can use a syllable in a word you know to help you read an unknown word.

par**rot**   **carrot**

Read each riddle. Look at the syllables in the words in bold print and write the two-syllable word that fits each clue.

1. It starts like **carry**.
   It ends like **parrot**.
   It grows in the ground.

   The word is _____.

2. It starts like **ago**.
   It ends like **belong**.
   It means "together with."

   The word is _____.

3. It starts like **robber**.
   It ends like **cabin**.
   It's a spring bird.

   The word is _____.

4. It starts like **bunny**.
   It ends like **puddle**.
   It's often wrapped up.

   The word is _____.

5. It starts like **asleep**.
   It ends like **depart**.
   It means "not together."

   The word is _____.

6. It starts like **metric**.
   It ends like **petal**.
   It's often shiny.

   The word is _____.

7. It starts like **candy**.
   It ends like **handle**.
   It's something you light.

   The word is _____.

8. It starts like **circle**.
   It ends like **focus**.
   It's a great show.

   The word is _____.

9. It starts like **dragging**.
   It ends like **wagon**.
   It's sometimes mechanical.

   The word is _____.

PHONICS Alive at Home
Together, complete this riddle:
It starts like **penny**. It ends like **stencil**.

Name _____

Read the magazine article about a new invention. Think about why and how the invention came to be. Then answer the questions.

Cricket Corral:
A Neat Idea

Picture this scene.

It's 4:00 P.M.—time to feed Tina, your pet toad. You open a box of fresh crickets from the pet store. You grab a bunch of the big bugs. They squirm and kick. A few escape into your living room.

Can anything be done about messy mealtimes like these? David Rose and Darby Cunningham thought so. The two inventors recently received a patent for a device they call the "Cricket Corral."

Here's how the invention works. You fill a container with crickets. Then you put on the lid, which has a wide tube sticking out of it. Some of the crickets climb into the tube.

When you're ready to feed your pet, just lift out the tube and give it a tap. The crickets fall out. You don't have to touch them. Now that's neat!

I. What made David Rose and Darby Cunningham invent the Cricket Corral?

_____

_____

2. How does the invention work?

_____

_____

_____

Read and Write

Suppose you could interview the inventors of the Cricket Corral. What would you ask? Write three or four questions. Use one or more words from the box.

Writer's Tips

- Stick to the topic. Ask questions that have to do with the invention and being an inventor.
- Use the information in the article to help you write your questions.
- Make your questions count. Try to get lots of information.

| able |
| admire |
| apply |
| create |
| device |
| ever |
| famous |
| item |
| money |
| patent |
| people |
| problem |

Ask your child to read his or her interview questions to you. Make up answers to the questions.

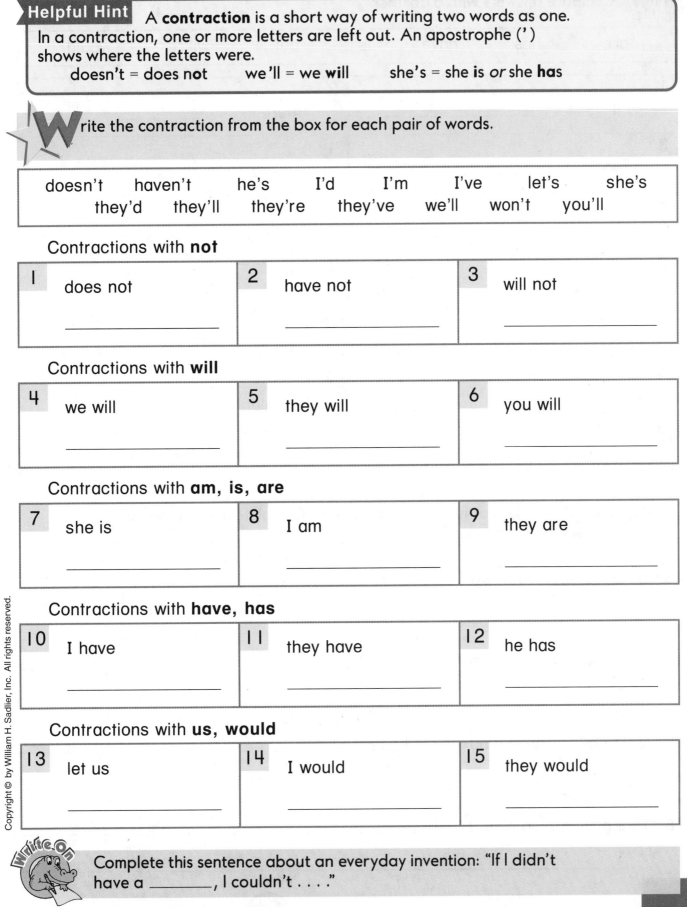

Name _____

Helpful Hint A **contraction** is a short way of writing two words as one. In a contraction, one or more letters are left out. An apostrophe (') shows where the letters were.

doesn't = does n**ot**   we'll = we **will**   she's = she **is** *or* she **ha**s

Write the contraction from the box for each pair of words.

doesn't	haven't	he's	I'd	I'm	I've	let's	she's
they'd	they'll	they're	they've	we'll	won't	you'll	

Contractions with **not**

1 does not	2 have not	3 will not
_____	_____	_____

Contractions with **will**

4 we will	5 they will	6 you will
_____	_____	_____

Contractions with **am, is, are**

7 she is	8 I am	9 they are
_____	_____	_____

Contractions with **have, has**

10 I have	11 they have	12 he has
_____	_____	_____

Contractions with **us, would**

13 let us	14 I would	15 they would
_____	_____	_____

Complete this sentence about an everyday invention: "If I didn't have a _____, I couldn't . . . ."

LESSON 75: Recognizing and Writing Contractions

133

Write the words for each contraction. Use one of the words from the box. Compare answers with a partner.

are	has	have	is	not	will	would

1 I'll _____		2 there's _____	
3 we'd _____		4 you're _____	
5 it's _____		6 can't _____	
7 wasn't _____		8 don't _____	
9 isn't _____		10 you've _____	
11 we've _____		12 shouldn't _____	
13 couldn't _____		14 that's _____	

What's there to do at home on a rainy day? Complete each sentence using a contraction.

15. It rained yesterday, so _____

_____

16. I wanted to have fun, but _____

_____

17. Mom said, "I have a box in the basement that _____

_____

18. That gave me an idea. I built _____

_____

LESSON 75: Recognizing and Writing Contractions

Ask your child to circle the contraction in each sentence and to name the words for each contraction.

Name _____

Read the selection about an accidental invention. Underline the contractions and write the words for the contractions below.

What's shaped like a pig and holds coins? It's a piggy bank, of course. You might think a piggy bank gets its name from its shape, but that's not the case. Here's the story of how little pigs became banks.

In England during the 1400's, jars and pots weren't made from glass or metal. That wouldn't have been practical. Potters used a clay called "pygg" instead. People soon called the jar in which they put their spare change a "pygg jar" or "pygg bank."

As time passed, people didn't remember that pygg was clay. At some point, a potter asked to make a "pygg bank" must have made a bank shaped like a pig. Wasn't that a great mistake! Piggy banks are still popular today.

_____   _____

_____   _____

_____   _____

What do you think would be a good shape for a coin bank? Write a sentence or two explaining your choice.

_____

_____

_____

 **Check-Up** Write the contraction for each pair of words.

1. is not _____	2. let us _____
3. she is _____	4. do not _____
5. you will _____	6. they are _____
7. we have _____	8. it has _____
9. I would _____	10. there is _____

Write the words for each contraction.

11. haven't _____	12. doesn't _____
13. they'd _____	14. you've _____
15. couldn't _____	16. they'll _____
17. that's _____	18. won't _____

Circle the contraction in each sentence. Then write the words for the contraction.

19. "I've got a problem," said Julia. _____

20. "What's wrong?" asked her friend Kim. _____

21. "I'm always losing my pencils," Julia replied. _____

22. "They're never where I leave them." _____

23. "Why don't we work together?" asked Kim. _____

24. "We'll invent something to help you." _____

Helpful Hint **Plural** means "more than one." Add **s** to most **base words** to make plurals. Add **es** to words that end in **s, ss, ch, sh, x,** or **z.**

bag + **s** = bag**s**   dress + **es** = dress**es**

Add **s** or **es** to write the plural of each base word.

1	bag _____	2	dress _____
3	ax _____	4	lake _____
5	watch _____	6	bus _____

Write the base word.

7	foxes _____	8	guesses _____
9	wishes _____	10	shells _____
11	cones _____	12	porches _____

Add **s** or **es** to each word in bold print so that the sentence makes sense. Write the new word.

13. Will you help me unpack these **box**?   _____

14. You can stack the cans of **peach.**   _____

15. The **bottle** of juice go on the shelf.   _____

16. Now let's make some picnic **lunch.**   _____

17. Here's a jar of jam and four **slice** of bread.   _____

18. I'll put two **glass** in the picnic basket.   _____

19. We'll toast the person who invented **sandwich.**   _____

Helpful Hint When a base word ends in **y** after a consonant, change the **y** to **i** before adding **es**. When the **y** follows a vowel, just add **s**.

story + **es** = stor**ies**   toy + **s** = toy**s**

Write the plural of each base word.

1	story _____	2	toy _____
3	family _____	4	day _____
5	boy _____	6	turkey _____

Write the base word.

7	cherries _____	8	rays _____
9	trays _____	10	pennies _____
11	groceries _____	12	chimneys _____

Add **s** or **es** to a base word from the box to answer each question.

berry	buddy	city	jay	key	monkey	pony

13. What do you use to open locks? _____

14. What animals look like small horses? _____

15. What are small, juicy fruits with seeds? _____

16. What are noisy, blue birds? _____

17. Where would you find skyscrapers? _____

18. What animals are related to apes? _____

19. What are best friends? _____

With your child, take turns reading the questions and answers at the bottom of the page.

Name _____

Helpful Hint   When a base word ends in **f** or **fe**, change **f** or **fe** to **v** and add **es**.
scar**f** + **es** = scar**ves**   kni**fe** + **es** = kni**ves**

⭐ **W**rite the plural of the base word to name each picture.

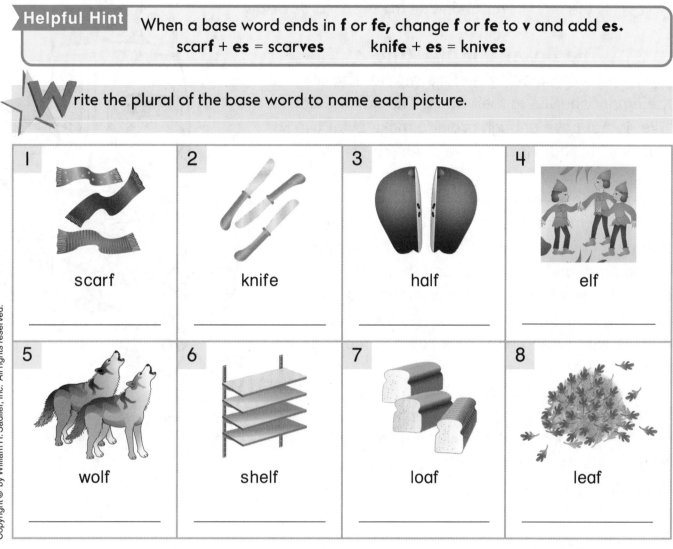

1 scarf	2 knife	3 half	4 elf
_____	_____	_____	_____
5 wolf	6 shelf	7 loaf	8 leaf
_____	_____	_____	_____

Work Together   Write the plural of the base word to complete each sentence. Take turns naming the plurals and reading the sentences with a partner.

knife   9. Did you know that the first _____ were made of stone?

loaf   10. The first plates were made from _____ of bread.

shelf   11. People did not store things on _____ until the Middle Ages.

hoof   12. The Romans invented horseshoes to protect horses' _____ .

calf   13. Before barbed wire was invented, thorny bushes were used to

fence in _____ .

leaf   14. Two brothers invented the leaf-pusher to scoop _____ from a swimming pool.

Read about the baker and his wife. Underline the plural words that end in **ves** and write the base words below.

The Baker and His Wife

One evening a baker and his wife looked at the empty shelves in their shop. The baker said, "We do not have enough grain to make even two loaves of bread. How can we open tomorrow?"

"Do not worry," said his wife. "We've led charmed lives. We'll work it out."

"You're the best of wives," said the baker. "Let's go home." They put away the bowls, the rolling pins, and the knives, and they left.

On the way home, the baker stopped short. "We forgot to lock up," he said. So the baker and his wife turned back. The lights in the shop were blazing.

"Oh no!" cried the baker. "We're being robbed by thieves dressed in green suits and red scarves."

"They look like elves to me," said his wife. "But what's that contraption? I've never seen anything like it."

_____ _____ _____ _____

_____ _____ _____ _____

What happens next? Continue the story.

_____

_____

_____

_____

_____

_____

LESSON 79: Adding Plural Ending **es** to Words Ending in **f** and **fe**

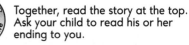

Together, read the story at the top. Ask your child to read his or her ending to you.

Helpful Hint An apostrophe and an **s** (**'s**) can be added to the end of a word to show ownership.

the tools that belong to **Maria** = **Maria's** tools
the idea of one **person** = one **person's** idea

Rewrite each phrase. Add **'s** to the word in bold print to show who owns something.

1. the cat that belongs to **Michael** _____

2. the wagon of **Anita** _____

3. the collar on my **dog** _____

4. the opinion of an **expert** _____

5. the hard drive of the **computer** _____

Work Together Circle the phrases that show ownership. Then use each circled phrase in a sentence. Share your sentences with a partner.

Beth's invention	the dog's toy	three pencils
Jed's gadget	plates of food	the clock's hands
green leaves	Mom's keys	hearing aids

6. _____

   _____

7. _____

   _____

8. _____

   _____

9. _____

   _____

10. _____

   _____

Rewrite each phrase. Add an apostrophe (') to the plural word in bold print to show who owns something.

1. the books that belong to my **sisters** _____

2. the inventions of the **scientists** _____

3. the branches of the **trees** _____

4. the feathers on the **birds** _____

5. the rackets that belong to the **players** _____

6. the shoes of the **runners** _____

7. the voices of the **teachers** _____

8. the game that belongs to my **brothers** _____

Circle the word that completes each sentence. Choose the word with **s'** when you want to show ownership.

9. My friends and I are starting a ___ club. | kids | kids'

10. It's for ___ who like to invent things. | kids | kids'

11. The first two ___ will take place at my house. | meetings | meetings'

12. Then we'll take turns meeting at other ___ houses. | members | members'

13. We've already put together a list of ___. | tools | tools'

14. We'll gather the tools and other ___. | materials | materials'

15. Then we'll get started on a variety of ___. | projects | projects'

16. Don't worry! We'll work under our ___ supervision. | parents | parents'

What kind of kids' club would you join? Write a sentence or two to tell about it.

Together, replace the plural words in items 1–8 to change ownership, for example, **my friends' books.**

Name _____

Add **s, es, 's,** or **s'** to each base word and write a word to complete each sentence. Remember to make spelling changes. Then read the stories of two interesting inventions.

The Lock and the Key

Can you imagine carrying around _____ that
(key)

are over a foot long? That's what you would have done if you

were a wealthy Egyptian 4,000 _____ ago.
(year)

The _____ invented wooden locks with gigantic
(Egyptian)

keys to keep out _____. The Greeks borrowed
(thief)

the _____ idea and passed it on to the Romans.
(Egyptian)

The Ice Cream Cone

It happened in 1904 at the _____ Fair in
(World)

St. Louis. Ernest Hamwi was selling _____ next
(waffle)

to an ice cream vendor. The ice cream vendor ran out of

_____. Mr. Hamwi quickly rolled a waffle into a
(dish)

cone to hold a scoop of his _____ ice cream.
(neighbor)

That day Mr. Hamwi earned the _____ of
(thank)

_____ and friends from all over the world.
(family)

Check-Up Write the plural of each base word. Remember to make spelling changes.

1 buddy _____	2 wolf _____
3 key _____	4 bus _____
5 peach _____	6 day _____
7 party _____	8 dish _____
9 life _____	10 box _____

Write the base word.

11 shelves _____	12 foxes _____
13 boys _____	14 stories _____
15 bunnies _____	16 lunches _____
17 loaves _____	18 ponies _____

Rewrite each phrase. Use **'s** or an apostrophe (**'**) to show ownership.

19. the cows that belong to the farmer _____

20. the windows of the houses _____

21. the dog that belongs to Jamal _____

22. the tails on the bunnies _____

23. the panda that lives at the zoo _____

24. the hats of the girls _____

LESSON 82: Assessing Plurals and Possessives

 Review this Check-Up with your child.

Name _____

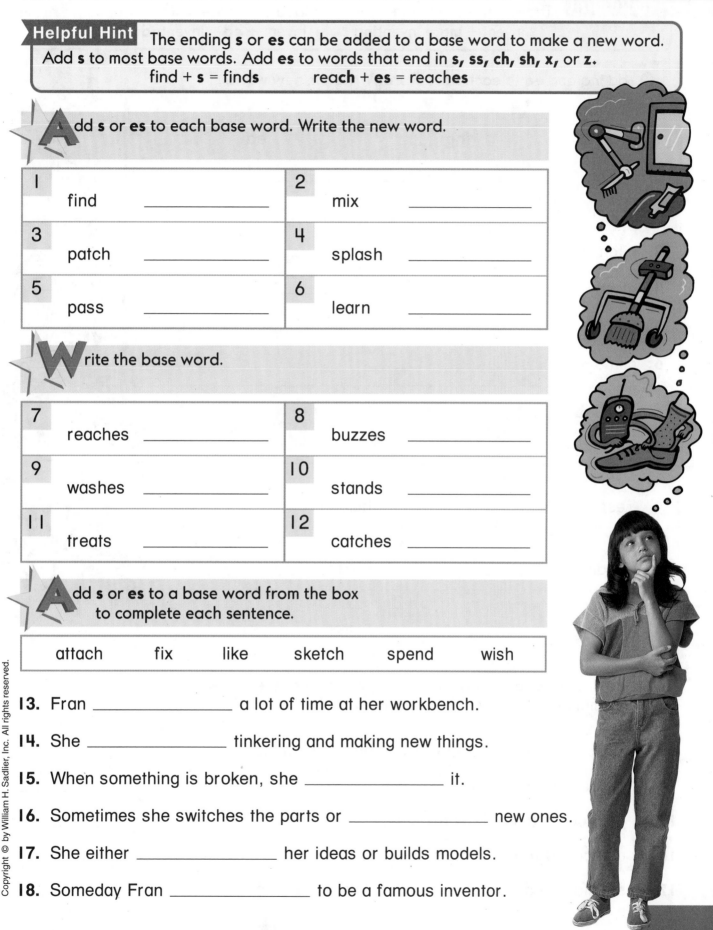

Helpful Hint The ending **s** or **es** can be added to a base word to make a new word. Add **s** to most base words. Add **es** to words that end in **s, ss, ch, sh, x,** or **z.**

find + **s** = find**s**   rea**ch** + **es** = reach**es**

Add **s** or **es** to each base word. Write the new word.

1 find _____		2 mix _____	
3 patch _____		4 splash _____	
5 pass _____		6 learn _____	

Write the base word.

7 reaches _____		8 buzzes _____	
9 washes _____		10 stands _____	
11 treats _____		12 catches _____	

Add **s** or **es** to a base word from the box to complete each sentence.

attach	fix	like	sketch	spend	wish

13. Fran _____ a lot of time at her workbench.

14. She _____ tinkering and making new things.

15. When something is broken, she _____ it.

16. Sometimes she switches the parts or _____ new ones.

17. She either _____ her ideas or builds models.

18. Someday Fran _____ to be a famous inventor.

LESSON 83: Writing Words with Inflectional Endings **s** and **es**

145

Add **ing** and **ed** to each base word. Write the new words.

	ing	ed
1. invent	_____	_____
2. splash	_____	_____
3. pitch	_____	_____
4. start	_____	_____
5. march	_____	_____
6. climb	_____	_____

Write the base word.

7 rested _____	8 helped _____
9 reading _____	10 holding _____
11 pushing _____	12 listed _____

Add **ing** or **ed** to each word in bold print so that the sentence makes sense. Write the new word.

13. Is your cat always **scratch** to get out of the house? _____

14. Consider **invent** a pet door. _____

15. A pet door is a small **swing** door. _____

16. It can be **attach** by hinges on the top. _____

17. It should swing shut after your pet has **pass** through. _____

With your child, look in a newspaper or book for words that end in **ing** and **ed**.

Name _____

Helpful Hint When a base word ends in **y** after a consonant, change the **y** to **i** before adding **es** or **ed**. When the **y** follows a vowel, just add **s** or **ed**.

carry + es = carries   carry + ed = carried
play + s = plays   play + ed = played

Add the endings to each base word. Write the new words.

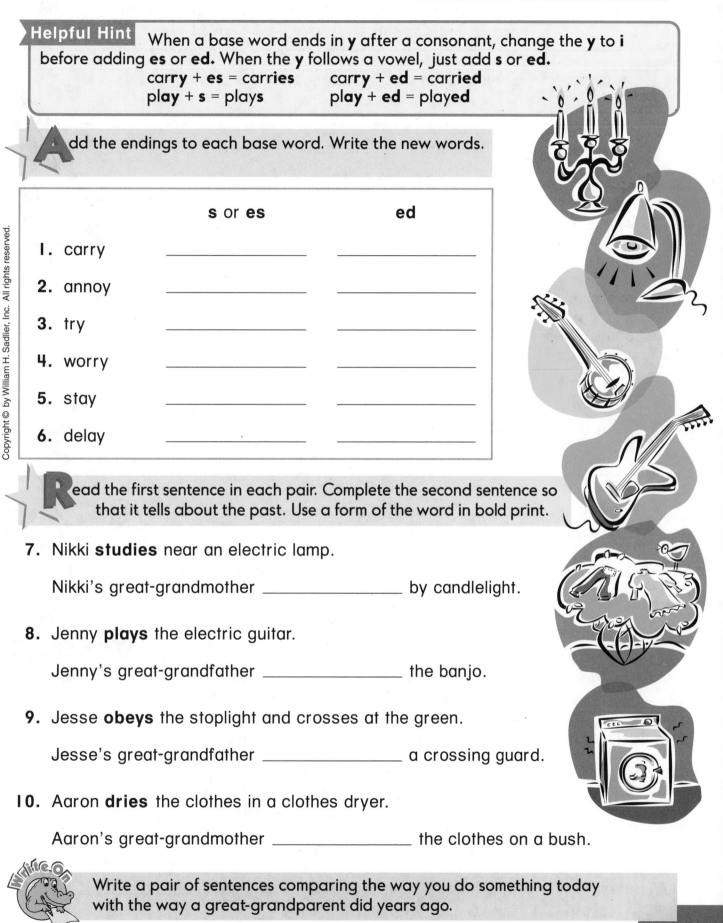

	s or es	ed
1. carry	_____	_____
2. annoy	_____	_____
3. try	_____	_____
4. worry	_____	_____
5. stay	_____	_____
6. delay	_____	_____

Read the first sentence in each pair. Complete the second sentence so that it tells about the past. Use a form of the word in bold print.

7. Nikki **studies** near an electric lamp.

   Nikki's great-grandmother _____ by candlelight.

8. Jenny **plays** the electric guitar.

   Jenny's great-grandfather _____ the banjo.

9. Jesse **obeys** the stoplight and crosses at the green.

   Jesse's great-grandfather _____ a crossing guard.

10. Aaron **dries** the clothes in a clothes dryer.

    Aaron's great-grandmother _____ the clothes on a bush.

Write a pair of sentences comparing the way you do something today with the way a great-grandparent did years ago.

Drop the final **e** and add **ing** and **ed** to each base word. Write the new words.

	ing	ed
1. save	_____	_____
2. wipe	_____	_____
3. hope	_____	_____
4. exercise	_____	_____
5. paste	_____	_____
6. sneeze	_____	_____

Write the base word.

7 waving _____	8 practiced _____
9 cared _____	10 tracing _____
11 erasing _____	12 joked _____

Add **ing** or **ed** to each word in bold print so that the sentence makes sense. Write the new word.

13. In 1760 Joseph Merlin **create** a pair of wheeled shoes. _____

14. When he rolled into a party, he **startle** the other guests. _____

15. Unable to stop or steer, he **skate** right into a mirror. _____

16. That might have ended the story of roller **skate**. _____

17. But another inventor found a way of **improve** the skates. _____

Ask your child to read the corrected sentences at the bottom to you.

Name _____

Helpful Hint When a short vowel word ends in a single consonant, usually double the final consonant before adding **ing** or **ed.**

ski**p** + **ing** = ski**pping**   ski**p** + **ed** = ski**pped**

Double the final consonant and add **ing** and **ed** to each base word. Write the new words.

	ing	**ed**
1. skip	_____	_____
2. grin	_____	_____
3. drip	_____	_____
4. tug	_____	_____
5. ship	_____	_____
6. clap	_____	_____
7. knot	_____	_____

Read one inventor's log. Circle each word ending in **ing** or **ed.** Write the base word.

Monday: went jogging with Joe _____

Tuesday: tapped maple trees for syrup _____

Wednesday: canned string beans _____

Thursday: went shopping with Elana _____

Friday: went swimming and came up with an idea for a machine _____

Work with a small group to invent a swimming machine. Jot down your ideas. Share your plans with classmates.

LESSON 86: Doubling Final Consonant Before Adding Inflectional Ending **ing** or **ed**

149

Helpful Hint Every **syllable** has a vowel sound. Sometimes an ending has a vowel sound and forms a syllable. Sometimes it does not.

uses—**2** vowel sounds—**2** syllables
used—**1** vowel sound—**1** syllable

Read each phrase. Circle the word ending in **s, es, ing,** or **ed.**
Then write the word under the correct heading.

	One Syllable	Two Syllables
1. often uses scrap material	_____	_____
2. builds a model	_____	_____
3. might have caused a problem	_____	_____
4. added a new part	_____	_____
5. start making a plan	_____	_____
6. usually works on a team	_____	_____
7. carefully studies the problem	_____	_____
8. stopped to think	_____	_____
9. wanted to help	_____	_____
10. used a new method	_____	_____
11. makes a discovery	_____	_____
12. sketches an idea	_____	_____
13. first started to experiment	_____	_____
14. got wrapped up in her work	_____	_____
15. will be changing the world	_____	_____

Write a sentence using a two-syllable word with an ending.
Share your sentence with a partner.

_____

LESSON 87: Syllables in Words with Inflectional Endings

Ask your child to read to you all the
two-syllable words on the page.

Name _____

Add the ending to each base word and write the new word. Remember to make spelling changes. Then read down to find the answer to the question.

1. chat + s _____ _____ _____ _____

2. hatch + es _____ _____ _____ _____ _____ _____

3. dry + ed _____ _____ _____ _____

4. stay + s _____ _____ _____ _____

5. try + s _____ _____ _____ _____

6. play + ed _____ _____ _____ _____

7. hum + ed _____ _____ _____ _____

8. drip + ing _____ _____ _____ _____ _____ _____

9. hope + ed _____ _____ _____ _____

10. smile + ing _____ _____ _____ _____ _____

11. cry + ing _____ _____ _____ _____

12. plan + ed _____ _____ _____ _____ _____

13. name + ed _____ _____ _____ _____

It's fun jumping and bouncing on this invention.
What is it?

_____

Learn more about this invention. Find out when it was invented and by whom. Write about it.

Add **s, es, ing,** or **ed** to each base word and write a word to complete each sentence. Remember to make spelling changes. Then read the stories of two important inventions.

The Light Bulb

Was it American Thomas Edison or Englishman

Joseph Swan who _____ the light bulb?
(invent)

The answer to the question _____ on
(depend)

whether you live in America or England. Each inventor

on his own _____ and found a way to
(try)

keep an electric light _____. So credit
(burn)

_____ to both inventors.
(belong)

The Traffic Light

Believe it or not, the first traffic light was

_____ for horses, not cars! One was
(invent)

installed in England in 1868 to keep horse carriages

from _____ people. The idea seemed good,
(hit)

but the light soon _____. Fifty years
(explode)

_____ before American Garret Morgan
(pass)

_____ a traffic light that worked.
(patent)

152

LESSON 88: Reviewing Inflectional Endings

Ask your child to read the stories to you and to point out the ending in each word he or she wrote.

Name _____

Spell, Write, and Tell Read the phrases in the box. Say and spell each word in bold print. Repeat the word. Then sort the words.

annoyed by constant dripping

carries a backpack

sliced and **chopped** the onions

dries in just minutes

instantly **grows** ten feet

always **hoped** for the best

has **invented** something new

planning a party

reaches even into far corners

saving time and money

good for **scrubbing** pans

on sale **starting** now

never **tried** before

used for the first time

No Base Changes

_____

_____

_____

_____

_____

Change **y** to **i**

_____

_____

_____

Drop Final **e**

_____

_____

_____

Double Final Consonant

_____

_____

_____

Spell, Write, and Tell

Choose a simple invention that is used every day, and pretend that it's just been invented. Write a radio ad in which you describe the object and tell why people should buy it. In your ad, use one or more of your spelling words. Present the ad to classmates.

annoyed	carries	chopped	dries	grows	hoped	invented
planning	reaches	saving	scrubbing	starting	tried	used

LESSON 89: Connecting Spelling, Writing, and Speaking

Ask your child to present his or her ad. Together, look for words that end in **s, es, ed,** and **ing.**

Name _____

Read the how-to article. Think about the steps for becoming an inventor. Then answer the questions.

HOW TO BE AN Inventor

Use your brain and your imagination, and you can be an inventor. Here's how.

First, look for problems that need to be solved. For example, your CDs always fall on the floor, or your socks get mixed up in the wash. Brainstorm a list of possibilities.

Once you have a list, pick a problem to solve. Carefully think it over. Write down all possible solutions that pop into your head.

Now look at each solution. Cross out the ones that are silly or won't work. Circle the one that you'd like to try.

Make a drawing of your invention. List materials that you will need to make it. Then build a model with an adult's help.

When your model is done, try it out. If it works, you're an inventor!

I. What is the first step in becoming an inventor?

_____

_____

2. What should you do after you decide how to solve your problem?

_____

_____

LESSON 90: Connecting Reading and Writing
Comprehension: Identifying Steps in a Process

Follow the steps to become an inventor. Decide on and plan an invention. Then complete this application for a patent. Use one or more words from the box.

Writer's Tips

- Follow the directions for completing the application.
- Be precise. Make sure your reader understands what your invention does, who would use it, and how it works.
- Write neatly.

APPLICATION FOR A PATENT

To Whom It May Concern:

I, _____ , a resident of _____ , _____ ,
　　　　　[name]　　　　　　　　　　　　　　[city]　　　　　　[state]

have invented _____ .
　　　　　　　　　　　[name of invention]

Purpose of Invention
Explain what your invention does and who would use it.

_____

_____

_____

_____

Description of Invention
Draw a picture of your invention in the space at the left.
Tell how it works.

_____

_____

_____

_____

_____

I hereby apply for a patent.

Respectfully submitted,

_____　　　_____
　　　[signature]　　　　　　　　　　　[date]

| added |
| adult's |
| attached |
| families |
| fixes |
| I'd |
| improves |
| inventing |
| kids' |
| lunches |
| solves |
| toys |

156

LESSON 90: Connecting Reading and Writing
Comprehension: Identifying Steps in a Process

Ask your child to read his or her completed application to you, and to explain how to become an inventor.

Name _____

Let's read and talk about a camp for inventors of the future.

Are you interested in the world of inventors? If your answer is "yes," you may want to go to Camp Invention. This camp is a summer day camp for people who like to solve problems.

Camp Invention has different activity programs. In one, you'll get a chance to look at a few artists' work. For example, you can study Alexander Calder's mobiles to find out about metal objects moving in space. Then you'll have time to make a mobile of your own.

"What's Bugging You?" is another fun-filled program. While you're making a giant bug, you'll be learning about insects' habits. What you discover may be useful to humans in the future.

Camp Invention is going to be held in dozens of science centers and schools this summer. Maybe there will be one near you.

Would you like to attend Camp Invention? What else would you like to know about the summer program?

Check-Up Add **s** or **es, ing,** and **ed** to each base word. Write the new words. Remember to make spelling changes.

	s or es	ing	ed
1. splash	_____	_____	_____
2. learn	_____	_____	_____
3. wave	_____	_____	_____
4. study	_____	_____	_____
5. scrub	_____	_____	_____
6. obey	_____	_____	_____

Write the base word.

7 reaches _____	8 copies _____
9 baking _____	10 slipped _____
11 hurried _____	12 traces _____

Add **ing** or **ed** to the base word to complete each sentence.

live   **13.** Mary Anderson _____ in Birmingham, Alabama.

visit   **14.** Some say that in 1902 she _____ New York City.

enjoy   **15.** For the most part, she _____ her visit.

ride   **16.** But she didn't like _____ in trolleys on rainy days.

stop   **17.** It was impossible for the driver to wipe the windshields

without _____.

solve   **18.** Ms. Anderson was good at _____ problems.

invent   **19.** She _____ a windshield wiper.

 Review this Check-Up with your child.

Space Campers' Song

3—2—1— and liftoff,
Campers, off we go!
Departing from the planet Earth,
We're fearless, don't you know?

Weightless as we rocket
Soaring in the sky,
Where nothing is impossible
And anyone can fly,

Adventurers in outer space
Where galaxies do churn—
But don't forget about me, Mom,
In two weeks, I return.

Anastasia Suen

Critical Thinking

What do you think is possible in outer space?

How do you think it feels to fly among the galaxies?

LESSON 92: Suffixes, Prefixes, and Multisyllabic Words
Poetry: Rhyme

Dear Family,

In this unit about outer space, your child will learn about suffixes, prefixes, and multisyllabic words. Share these definitions:

suffix: a word part added to the end of a base word to change its meaning or make a new word (**hope<u>ful</u>**)

prefix: a word part added to the beginning of a base word to change its meaning or make a new word (**<u>re</u>tell**)

• Read the poem on the reverse side. Talk about adventures a space camper has.

• Ask your child to find the rhyming words, such as **go** and **know,** at the end of each pair of lines.

• Also search through the poem for words with suffixes, words with prefixes, and words with more than one syllable.

Apreciada Familia:

En esta unidad sobre el espacio los niños aprenderán sufijos, prefijos y palabras polisílabas. Compartan las siguientes definiciones:

sufijo: letras que se añaden al final de una palabra base para cambiar su significado o hacer una nueva (**hope<u>ful</u>**)

prefijo: letras que se añaden al principio de una palabra base para cambiar su significado o construir una nueva (**<u>re</u>tell**)

• Lean el poema en la página 159. Hablen de las aventuras en el campamento espacial.

• Pida al niño encontrar al final de cada verso palabras que riman tales como **go** y **know.**

• Busquen también palabras con sufijos y prefijos y palabras con más de una sílaba.

PROJECT

Use tissue boxes to design two space stations. Mark one box "Space Station Suffix" and the other "Prefix Planet Port." When your child learns a new word with a suffix or a prefix, have him or her write the word on a slip of paper, underline the suffix or prefix, and then place the paper in the appropriate space station.

PROYECTO

Usen cajas de pañuelos desechables para diseñar dos estaciones espaciales. Marquen una "Estación Espacial Sufijo" y la otra "Puerto Planeta Prefijo". Cuando el niño aprenda una palabra con sufijo o prefijo pídale escribirla en un papel, subrayar el sufijo o prefijo y luego colocarla en la estación espacial adecuada.

Helpful Hint A **suffix** is a word part added to the **end** of a base word to change its meaning or make a new word.

hope + **ful** = hope**ful**   bright + **ly** = bright**ly**   near + **er** = near**er**

The suffix **ful** means "full of," as in **hopeful**. The suffix **less** means "without," as in **hopeless**. The suffix **ness** means "a state of being," as in **darkness**. Add **ful, less,** or **ness** to the base word and write the word that goes with each definition.

1 full of **hope** _____	2 without **hope** _____	3 being **dark** _____
4 without **sun** _____	5 full of **cheer** _____	6 being **light** _____
7 being **good** _____	8 without **weight** _____	9 full of **color** _____

Add **ful, less,** or **ness** to each word in bold print so that the sentence makes sense. Write the new word.

10. The spacecraft took off on a **cloud** morning. _____

11. The **bright** of the sun lit up the sky. _____

12. The astronauts were **hope** that they would reach the moon. _____

13. Several days later they made a **grace** landing. _____

14. The brave astronauts were **fear** in the face of danger. _____

15. It's no wonder everyone praised their **great**. _____

The suffix **ly** means "in a certain way." **Brightly** means "in a bright way."
The suffix **y** means "full of" or "having." **Rainy** means "having rain."
Write the meaning of each word with **ly** or **y**.

1. brightly _____

2. rainy _____

3. safely _____

4. thirsty _____

5. speedy _____

6. clearly _____

7. snowy _____

8. completely _____

9. softly _____

Work with a partner. Add **ly** or **y** to the base word to answer
each question.

bright   10. How does the sun shine? _____

rock   11. What is the moon like? _____

quick   12. How do shooting stars move? _____

loud   13. How do crowds cheer? _____

salt   14. What is the ocean like? _____

dust   15. What is the planet Mars like? _____

brave   16. How does a space explorer act? _____

wind   17. What is a hurricane like? _____

slow   18. How does the moon travel around Earth? _____

Write two or three questions that can be answered with words
that end in **ly** or **y**.

With your child, take turns reading
the questions and answers at the
bottom of the page.

Name _____

Compare the sizes of the planets. Add **er** or **est** to the base word **big** and write the new word. Remember to make spelling changes.

Planet	Size Across in Miles
Uranus	31,800
Saturn	74,900
Jupiter	88,800

Uranus is a **big** planet.

1. Saturn is a _____ planet.

2. Jupiter is the _____ planet.

Add **er** and **est** to each base word. Write the new words. Remember to make spelling changes.

	er	est
3. easy	_____	_____
4. near	_____	_____
5. hot	_____	_____
6. high	_____	_____
7. sad	_____	_____
8. happy	_____	_____
9. early	_____	_____
10. thin	_____	_____

Find out about the sizes of the planets Mars, Mercury, and Pluto. Write three sentences comparing them. Use the words **small, smaller,** and **smallest.**

The suffix **en** means "make." **Darken** means "make dark." The suffixes **able** and **ible** mean "can be." **Washable** means "can be washed." **Collectible** means "can be collected." Write the meaning of each word with **en, able,** or **ible.**

1. darken _____

2. washable _____

3. collectible _____

4. soften _____

5. readable _____

6. sharpen _____

7. resistible _____

8. enjoyable _____

9. straighten _____

Write a word from above to complete each item on the list.

Things to Do at Space Camp

✔ Don't forget to _____ your bunk.

✔ Wash your clothes every week. They're all _____.

✔ _____ your pencils and write home often.

✔ Write neatly. Make sure your postcards are _____.

✔ Bring back moon rocks. They're _____.

✔ Have an _____ time.

With a classmate, make a list of collectibles, or things that can be collected. You might start your list with "moon rocks."

LESSON 95: Writing Suffixes **en, able, ible**

Together, look in a newspaper or book for words that end with the suffixes **en, able,** or **ible.**

Name _____

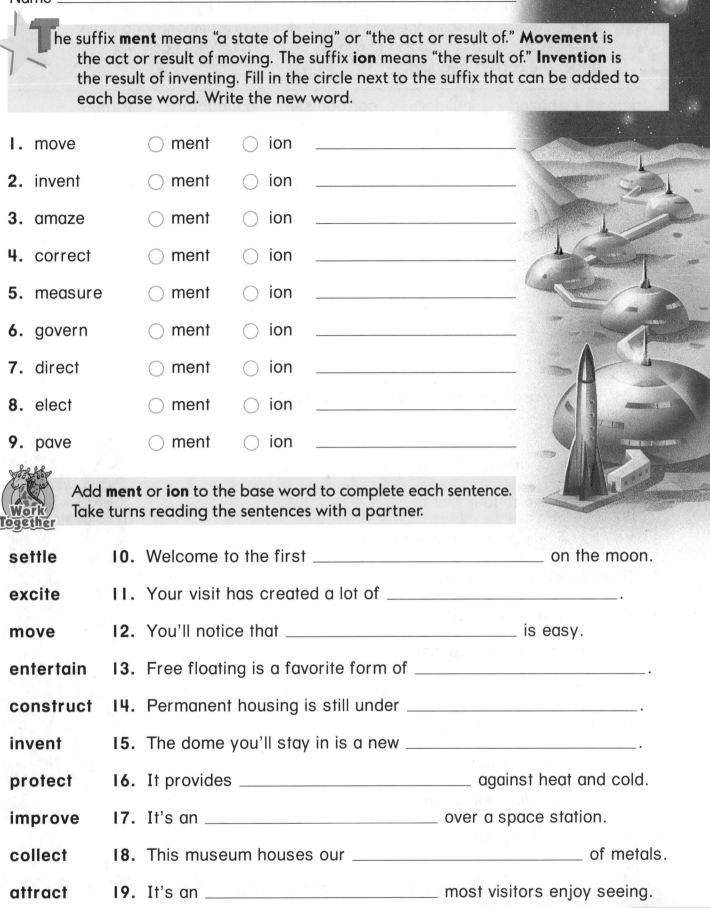

The suffix **ment** means "a state of being" or "the act or result of." **Movement** is the act or result of moving. The suffix **ion** means "the result of." **Invention** is the result of inventing. Fill in the circle next to the suffix that can be added to each base word. Write the new word.

1. move   ○ ment   ○ ion   _____

2. invent   ○ ment   ○ ion   _____

3. amaze   ○ ment   ○ ion   _____

4. correct   ○ ment   ○ ion   _____

5. measure   ○ ment   ○ ion   _____

6. govern   ○ ment   ○ ion   _____

7. direct   ○ ment   ○ ion   _____

8. elect   ○ ment   ○ ion   _____

9. pave   ○ ment   ○ ion   _____

Work Together

Add **ment** or **ion** to the base word to complete each sentence. Take turns reading the sentences with a partner.

settle   10. Welcome to the first _____ on the moon.

excite   11. Your visit has created a lot of _____.

move   12. You'll notice that _____ is easy.

entertain   13. Free floating is a favorite form of _____.

construct   14. Permanent housing is still under _____.

invent   15. The dome you'll stay in is a new _____.

protect   16. It provides _____ against heat and cold.

improve   17. It's an _____ over a space station.

collect   18. This museum houses our _____ of metals.

attract   19. It's an _____ most visitors enjoy seeing.

The suffixes **er, or,** and **ist** mean "someone who." A **farmer** is someone who farms. An **actor** is someone who acts. A **violinist** is someone who plays a violin. The words in the box end in **er, or,** and **ist.** Write each word under the correct heading.

actor	boxer	builder	cartoonist	conductor	farmer
inventor	journalist	sailor	teacher	tourist	violinist

1 Words with **er**	2 Words with **or**	3 Words with **ist**
_____	_____	_____
_____	_____	_____
_____	_____	_____
_____	_____	_____

Write the word from above that fits each clue.

4. He made the first telescope. _____

5. She would like to tour Mars. _____

6. You'll see this person in the movies. _____

7. This person grows vegetables. _____

8. She draws a comic strip. _____

9. He writes for the newspaper. _____

10. You'll see this person in the classroom. _____

11. This person leads an orchestra. _____

12. You'll see this person in a boxing ring. _____

13. This person plays the violin. _____

14. This person sails the seas. _____

Write a word with **er, or,** or **ist** that can be used to describe you.

Ask your child to write clues for the words **artist, director,** and **photographer.**

Name _____

You can use a suffix you know to help you read an unknown word.
ful   hope**ful**   thought**ful**

Say the suffix at the beginning of each row. Circle the words that end with the same suffix.

1	**ful**	hopeful	hoping	thoughtful	thoughtless
2	**less**	dampness	weightless	cheerful	shapeless
3	**ness**	pointless	closeness	sickness	tightest
4	**ly**	safely	safer	thirsty	sweetly
5	**y**	squeaky	kindly	rocky	rocket
6	**er**	lighter	louder	little	lightest
7	**est**	warmest	wanted	greatest	slower

Interview an astronaut. Write a circled word from above to complete each question. Use the suffix clues to help you. Then write two interview questions of your own.

less 8. How does it feel to be _____ in space?

ness 9. Did you ever experience motion _____?

est 10. What was your spacecraft's _____ speed?

er 11. Was the noise _____ during blastoff or touchdown?

y 12. Is the moon's surface really _____?

ly 13. How did you feel after landing _____?

ful 14. Are you _____ that someday we'll live in space?

15. _____

_____

16. _____

_____

LESSON 98: Syllables in Words with Suffixes **ful, less, ness, ly, y, er, est**

167

You can use a suffix you know to help you read an unknown word.
en   dark**en**   **able**   read**able**

Say each base word and suffix. Then add the suffix to the base word to write a new word.

1 light + en _____ bright + en _____	**2** bend + able _____ wear + able _____
3 collect + ible _____ resist + ible _____	**4** place + ment _____ agree + ment _____
5 subtract + ion _____ suggest + ion _____	**6** lead + er _____ sing + er _____
7 conduct + or _____ visit + or _____	**8** guitar + ist _____ novel + ist _____

Write a word from above to answer each question.

9. What two-syllable word is a kind of entertainer? _____

10. What three-syllable word is another word for **guest**? _____

11. What two-syllable word is the act of placing? _____

12. What three-syllable word is the opposite of **addition**? _____

13. What two-syllable word means "make light"? _____

14. What three-syllable word is an author? _____

15. What four-syllable word means "can be resisted"? _____

16. What three-syllable word means "can be bent"? _____

LESSON 98: Syllables in Words with Suffixes
en, able, ible, ment, ion, er, or, ist

Ask your child to point out the words he or she wrote in items 1–8 that have more than two syllables.

Read about some visitors from space. Then answer the questions.

Visitors from Space

It's a dark night. The stars are shining brightly. You hear a knock and open your door. To your amazement, in float several tourists from space. What might they be like? Before you guess, it would be helpful to know something about their home planet.

Let's say your visitors come from a snowy planet—perhaps the planet farthest from the sun. Then they might have hairy bodies for protection against the cold.

Let's say the travelers come from a large planet—one that has stronger gravity than Earth. Then they might feel almost weightless. They'd be light on their feet and able to jump higher than you.

Will they definitely have feet? It's questionable. What do you think?

---

1. Why might space visitors have hairy bodies?

_____

_____

2. How might coming from a large planet affect the visitors' movement on Earth?

_____

_____

3. Do you think it's possible for space visitors to be exactly like humans? Why or why not?

_____

_____

Write the base word and suffix for each word.

	Base Word	Suffix
1. measurement	_____	_____
2. weightless	_____	_____
3. breakable	_____	_____
4. inventor	_____	_____
5. collectible	_____	_____
6. tourist	_____	_____
7. darkness	_____	_____
8. teacher	_____	_____

Fill in the circle next to the word that makes sense in each sentence.

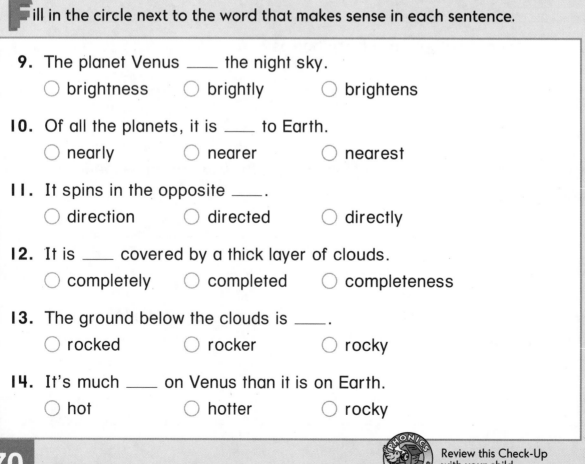

9. The planet Venus ___ the night sky.
   ○ brightness   ○ brightly   ○ brightens

10. Of all the planets, it is ___ to Earth.
    ○ nearly   ○ nearer   ○ nearest

11. It spins in the opposite ___.
    ○ direction   ○ directed   ○ directly

12. It is ___ covered by a thick layer of clouds.
    ○ completely   ○ completed   ○ completeness

13. The ground below the clouds is ___.
    ○ rocked   ○ rocker   ○ rocky

14. It's much ___ on Venus than it is on Earth.
    ○ hot   ○ hotter   ○ rocky

 Review this Check-Up with your child.

Name _____

> **Helpful Hint** A **prefix** is a word part added to the **beginning** of a base word to change its meaning or make a new word.
>
> **re** + tell = **re**tell   **in** + correct = **in**correct   **pre** + pay = **pre**pay

The prefix **re** means "again" or "back," as in **retell** and **return.** The prefixes **un** and **dis** mean "not" or "do the opposite of," as in **unsafe** and **disagree.** Add **re, un,** or **dis** to the base word and write the word that goes with each definition.

1 **tell** again _____	**2** not **honest** _____	**3** **turn** back _____
4 not **known** _____	**5** **build** again _____	**6** not **safe** _____
7 the opposite of **obey** _____	**8** the opposite of **load** _____	**9** the opposite of **agree** _____

Add **re, un,** or **dis** to each word in bold print so that the sentence makes sense. Write the new word.

10. I checked and then **checked** the facts.   _____

11. I worked hard to **cover** information.   _____

12. But my report on black holes **appeared**!   _____

13. I've looked, but I'm **able** to find it.   _____

14. My teacher **likes** excuses.   _____

15. I guess that I'll have to **write** it.   _____

The prefixes **in** and **im** mean "not." **Incorrect** means "not correct." **Impossible** means "not possible." Add **in** or **im** to each base word. Write the new word.

1	Add **in**	2	Add **im**
correct	_____	possible	_____
visible	_____	polite	_____
complete	_____	pure	_____
formal	_____	patient	_____
expensive	_____	perfect	_____
active	_____	mature	_____

Write a word from above to complete each sentence.
Compare answers with a partner.

3. A person who is not patient is _____.

4. A toy that is not expensive is _____.

5. Something that is not perfect is _____.

6. Someone who is not polite is _____.

7. A job that has not been completed is _____.

8. Something that cannot be seen is _____.

9. A volcano that is not active is _____.

10. Water that is not pure is _____.

11. An answer that is not correct is _____.

12. A person who is not mature is _____.

13. Something that is not possible is _____.

14. A party that is not formal is _____.

Write a sentence to describe something that is impossible on Earth, but possible in space.

LESSON 101: Writing Prefixes **in** and **im**

Together, rewrite the definition sentences above, for example: A coach who is not patient is impatient.

Name _____

The prefix **pre** means "before." **Prepay** means "pay before." The prefix **de** means "remove." **Defrost** means "remove frost from." The prefix **mis** means "in a wrong or bad way." **Misspell** means "spell in a wrong way." The words in the box begin with **pre, de,** and **mis.** Write each word under the correct heading.

| decode | defrost | mislabel | prepay | misspell | preview |
| defang | pretest | dethrone | mistreat | misuse | prewash |

1 Words with **pre**	2 Words with **de**	3 Words with **mis**
_____	_____	_____
_____	_____	_____
_____	_____	_____
_____	_____	_____

Write a word from above to complete each sentence.

4. When you test something in advance, you _____ it.

5. When you remove frost from a windshield, you _____ it.

6. When you treat a pet badly, you _____ it.

7. When you use a knife as a fork, you _____ it.

8. When you pay for something in advance, you _____.

9. When you remove or break a secret code, you _____.

10. When you wash something beforehand, you _____ it.

11. When you spell a word incorrectly, you _____ it.

12. When you remove the queen from her throne, you _____ her.

13. When you skim a book before reading it, you _____ it.

Write a sentence to explain why the word **prefix** begins with **pre.**

You can use a prefix you know to help you read an unknown word.

re   **re**check   **re**read

Say the prefix at the beginning of each row. Circle the words that begin with the same prefix.

1	**re**	redo	reread	preheat	defrost
2	**un**	ugly	unhappy	onion	unwrap
3	**dis**	describe	listen	dislike	displease
4	**in**	inactive	impolite	indirect	imperfect
5	**im**	impossible	inexpensive	improper	unknown
6	**pre**	preschool	retake	repay	prehistoric
7	**de**	debug	preview	declaw	distrust
8	**mis**	middle	disobey	mislead	mistook

Write a circled word from above to answer each question.

9. What two-syllable word means "read again"? _____

10. What three-syllable word is the opposite of **direct**? _____

11. What four-syllable word describes early times in history? _____

12. What two-syllable word means "remove the claws of"? _____

13. What three-syllable word is another word for **sad**? _____

14. What four-syllable word is the opposite of **possible**? _____

15. What two-syllable word is a form of the word **mistake**? _____

16. What two-syllable word is the opposite of **please**? _____

Sort the words with prefixes into three groups: Words with Two Syllables, Words with Three Syllables, Words with Four Syllables. Make three lists.

Ask your child to write questions about the words with prefixes that are not circled in items 1–8.

Name _____

Write a word with a prefix for each clue. Use a prefix from the box.
Then read down to find the answer to the question.

re	un	dis	in	im	pre	de	mis

1. cook before   __ __ __ __ __ __ __

2. not correct   __ __ __ __ __ __ __

3. the opposite of **cover**   __ __ __ __ __ __

4. spell in a wrong way   __ __ __ __ __ __ __

5. tell again   __ __ __ __ __ __

6. heat before   __ __ __ __ __ __

7. the opposite of **like**   __ __ __ __ __ __ __

8. remove the claws of   __ __ __ __ __

9. not patient   __ __ __ __ __ __ __

10. treat badly   __ __ __ __ __ __ __

11. not pure   __ __ __ __ __ __

12. remove the code   __ __ __ __ __

13. the opposite of **wrap**   __ __ __ __ __

14. the opposite of **obey**   __ __ __ __ __ __ __

What are groups of bright stars that form shapes in the sky?

_____

Check-Up Write the prefix and base word for each word.

	Prefix	Base Word
1. decode	_____	_____
2. misuse	_____	_____
3. disobey	_____	_____
4. prewash	_____	_____
5. impolite	_____	_____
6. unknown	_____	_____
7. invisible	_____	_____
8. rebuild	_____	_____

Fill in the circle next to the word that makes sense in each sentence.

9. The sun was formed in ___ times.
   ○ prehistoric   ○ inexpensive   ○ pretest

10. It's ___ to look directly at it.
   ○ unable   ○ unsafe   ○ impatient

11. It's ___ to live without it.
   ○ inactive   ○ unhappy   ○ impossible

12. During an eclipse, the sun seems to ___.
   ○ disagree   ○ declaw   ○ disappear

13. It ___ a few minutes later.
   ○ rechecks   ○ returns   ○ prepays

14. Long ago people ___ an eclipse for a dragon eating the sun!
   ○ mistook   ○ mistreat   ○ mislead

 Review this Check-Up with your child.

Helpful Hint If a word has two or more consonants between two vowels, usually divide the word between the first two consonants.
ex-pect   hun-dred
VC CV   VC CCV

Write each word, dividing it into syllables with a hyphen.

1 expect _____	2 hundred _____
3 surface _____	4 person _____
5 mission _____	6 shelter _____
7 success _____	8 surround _____
9 orbit _____	10 correct _____
11 common _____	12 surprise _____

Write a word from above to complete each sentence.

13. Cosmonaut Yuri Gagarin was the first _____ to circle Earth in 1961.

14. A year later astronaut John Glenn went into _____.

15. Seven years later Neil Armstrong went on a _____ to the moon.

16. Scientists _____ that in the future astronauts will visit other planets.

17. Someday space travel may become as _____ as airplane travel.

Helpful Hint If a word has one consonant between two vowels, first divide the word before the consonant. The first vowel sound will usually be long. If you still don't recognize the word, divide after the consonant. The vowel sound will usually be short.

fu-ture   p**lan-e**ts
V CV   VC V

Write each word, dividing it into syllables with a hyphen.

1	future _____	2	planets _____
3	nature _____	4	solar _____
5	cabin _____	6	metal _____
7	climate _____	8	silence _____
9	moment _____	10	frozen _____
11	panel _____	12	travel _____
13	shiver _____	14	models _____

Write a word from above to complete each sentence.
Take turns reading the sentences with a partner.

15. The science museum has exhibits on both past and _____ space flights.

16. One room is set up like the _____ of a spacecraft.

17. Visitors can sit behind the control _____ .

18. Another room displays all the planets in the _____ system.

19. The scale _____ are built to show the planets' sizes.

20. Jupiter is bigger than all the other _____ put together!

Name _____

Helpful Hint Divide a compound word between its word parts.
moon-walk **ice-berg**

Write each compound word, dividing it into syllables with a hyphen.

1 moonwalk _____	2 iceberg _____
3 blastoff _____	4 sunspot _____
5 spacesuit _____	6 daytime _____
7 postcard _____	8 footprints _____
9 daydream _____	10 touchdown _____
11 snowball _____	12 starlight _____
13 spacecraft _____	14 outside _____

Write the compound word from above that fits each clue.

15. This is a dark spot on the sun. _____

16. This is another word for **spaceship.** _____

17. This is a walk on the moon. _____

18. This is what Neil Armstrong left on the moon. _____

19. This is the launching of a spacecraft. _____

20. This is the landing of a spacecraft. _____

Find out why a comet is called "a dirty snowball."
Write a sentence or two about it.

LESSON 107: Syllabication in Compound Words

179

Read about a late night event. Underline the words in the selection that end in a consonant followed by **le.** Then write each underlined word below, dividing it into syllables with a hyphen.

A Star in the Night

It was the middle of the night. I looked up at the sky and saw a star twinkle. Suddenly a small object no bigger than a pebble fell to Earth. It landed with a splash in a puddle of rainwater. Something began to wriggle out.

It was quite a struggle! Finally, a tiny, fuzzy snake with two heads and a single body appeared. Each head looked like a round, blue marble. I tried not to startle the creature. I heard it gurgle softly.

Just then I felt Mom's gentle hand touch my cheek. I turned to point to the star snake with the double head.

_____   _____   _____

_____   _____   _____

_____   _____   _____

_____   _____   _____

What happens next? Continue the story.

_____

_____

_____

_____

Together, read the story at the top. Ask your child to read his or her ending to you.

Name _____

Helpful Hint If a word has an ending with a vowel sound, usually divide the word between the base word and the ending.

splash-**es**   thrill-**ing**   blast-**ed**

Write each word, dividing it into syllables with a hyphen.

1	splashes _____	2	thrilling _____
3	blasted _____	4	reaches _____
5	landed _____	6	touring _____
7	passes _____	8	wanted _____
9	flying _____	10	mixes _____
11	waited _____	12	missing _____
13	pushes _____	14	reading _____

Write a word from above to complete each sentence. Then read Davey's note.

Dear Mom and Dad,

I love _____ the solar system.

We're _____ at incredible speeds. By

the time this note _____ you, we'll have

_____ on Mars. You know I've always

_____ to leave my footprints there!

I'm having a blast!

Davey

Helpful Hint If a word has a suffix, usually divide the word between the base word and the suffix.

hope-**ful**   weight-**less**

Read each phrase and circle the word with a suffix. Then write the word, dividing it into syllables with a hyphen.

1. hopeful about the future _____

2. feel weightless in space _____

3. freeze in the darkness _____

4. bravely face the unknown _____

5. a rocky surface _____

6. smaller in size _____

7. the brightness of the stars _____

8. darken the skies _____

9. the movement of the planets _____

10. the best teacher _____

11. a sailor among the stars _____

12. a tourist on Earth _____

13. a rainless planet _____

14. the greatest distance _____

15. splash down safely _____

16. a graceful landing _____

17. a dirty snowball _____

18. sharpen the focus _____

How do you divide a word that ends with the suffix **able** or **ible**? Divide the word **readable.** Use what you know about suffixes and words that end in a consonant followed by **le.**

Together, scan a newspaper column for hyphenated words with suffixes. Notice how they are divided.

Name _____

Read each phrase and circle the word with a prefix. Then write the word, dividing it into syllables with a hyphen.

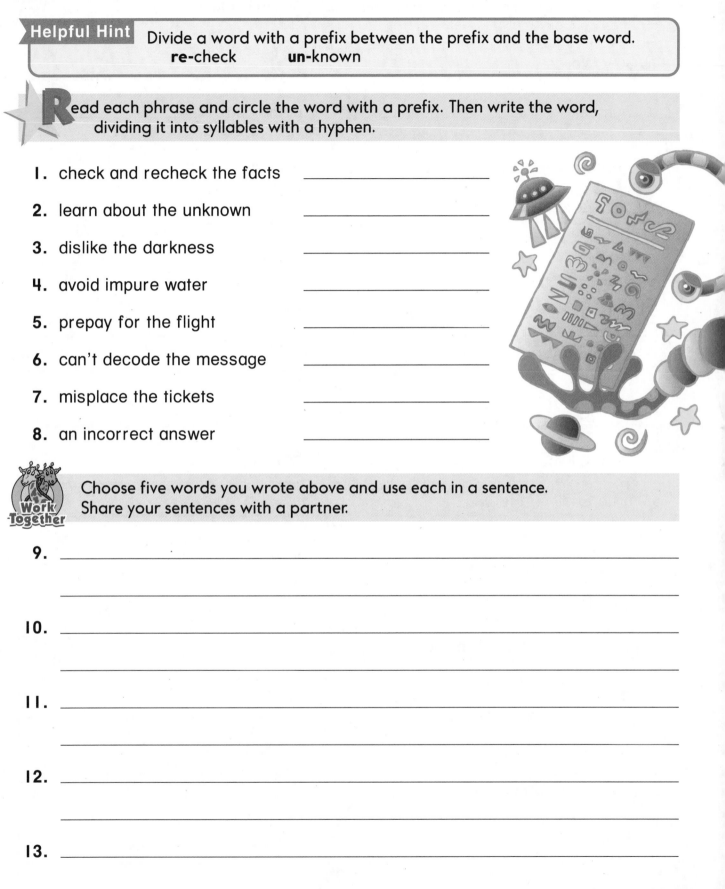

1. check and recheck the facts   _____

2. learn about the unknown   _____

3. dislike the darkness   _____

4. avoid impure water   _____

5. prepay for the flight   _____

6. can't decode the message   _____

7. misplace the tickets   _____

8. an incorrect answer   _____

Choose five words you wrote above and use each in a sentence. Share your sentences with a partner.

9. _____

_____

10. _____

_____

11. _____

_____

12. _____

_____

13. _____

_____

Write each word, dividing it into syllables with a hyphen.

VCCV Words

1	number _____	2	command _____
3	purpose _____	4	danger _____

VCV Words

5	travel _____	6	silence _____
7	nature _____	8	figure _____

Compound Words

9	spacecraft _____	10	fireworks _____
11	earthquake _____	12	daydream _____

Words Ending in **le**

13	pebble _____	14	giggle _____
15	people _____	16	single _____

Words Ending in **es, ing, ed**

17	matches _____	18	speeding _____
19	waited _____	20	headed _____

Words with Suffixes and Prefixes

21	artist _____	22	brighten _____
23	preview _____	24	rebuild _____

LESSON 112: Reviewing Multisyllabic Words

Ask your child to explain how he or she divided each set of words.

Name _____

Spell, Write, and Tell

Read the phrases in the box. Say and spell each word in bold print. Repeat the word. Then sort the words.

a **better** view

departing from Earth

disappear into a black hole

an **impossible** plan

invisible to the naked eye

the biggest **planet**

in **prehistoric** times

beyond the **solar** system

launched a **spaceship**

streaking across the sky

a good **suggestion**

the moon's rocky **surface**

a **twinkle** in the darkness

explore the **unknown**

Two Syllables	Three Syllables
_____	_____
_____	_____
_____	_____
_____	**Four Syllables**
_____	_____
_____	_____
_____	

Spell Write and Tell

Imagine that you've discovered a new planet. Write a speech in which you greet visitors to your planet and describe what they will see there. In your speech, use one or more of your spelling words. Deliver the speech to the class.

better	departing	disappear	impossible	invisible
planet	prehistoric	solar	spaceship	
streaking	suggestion	surface	twinkle	unknown

MEET THE ☆ STARS

Ask your child to deliver his or her speech. Accept the invitation to tour the new planet.

Name _____

Read the conversation between a passenger and a driver on a bus traveling in space. Think about what the passenger says. Then answer the questions.

Aboard the Space Bus

Passenger: Wow! I can't believe I'm a space traveler. It's thrilling to travel in space. Driver, what's the first stop?

Driver: Our spacecraft is scheduled to pass Mercury. Mercury is the hottest planet. Do you know why?

Passenger: Because it's nearest the sun. So I guess it's not safe to land there.

Driver: Right. After Mercury, our spaceship will travel toward Venus. Venus is the planet closest to Earth.

Passenger: Then can we go to Mars? I've heard that people live there.

Driver: That's doubtful, but we'll have an enjoyable visit, anyhow.

Passenger: Then can we go to Jupiter? It's bigger than all the other planets. And after that, can we go to—

Driver: Calm down, ma'am! Don't be impatient! It's impossible to visit all the planets in one trip. We need to return to Earth for more fuel.

1. What is the route of the Space Bus?

_____

_____

2. How does the passenger feel about this trip? How do you know?

_____

_____

Imagine that it's the year 3000. You and a friend are on a Space Bus, heading for vacation on a faraway planet. Write a conversation that you have. Use one or more words from the box.

Writer's Tips

- Talk about what you see or hear.
- Tell where you are headed.
- Use the kind of language that you use when you talk with friends.

Word Box
amazement
brightness
cloudless
colorful
easier
happiest
impossible
invisible
loudly
preview
tourist
windy

LESSON 114: Connecting Reading and Writing
Comprehension: Evaluating Characters

Together, read the conversation that your child wrote. Each of you can take a part.

Name _____

Let's read and talk about space shuttles.

You hear a noise louder than thunder.
The rocket carrying the space shuttle
rises. Quickly the rocket disappears
into a cloudless sky.

A space shuttle is a spacecraft that
can be used over and over. Since the
Columbia blasted off in 1981, there
have been several space-shuttle flights.
In 1983, Sally Ride was a crew member
on the shuttle *Challenger*. She became
the first American woman in space.

A shuttle can hold up to seven
people. It can carry about 65,000
pounds of equipment. Shuttle crew
members use this equipment to
perform experiments in space. They
check and recheck test results. They
launch satellites that gather and
send information to scientists on
Earth. Shuttle crews also capture
and fix broken satellites.

What would you like most
about being a crew member
on a space shuttle?

LESSON 115: Suffixes, Prefixes, and Multisyllabic Words in Context
Comprehension: Relating to Personal Experiences

Write each word, dividing it into syllables with a hyphen.

1 swiftly _____	2 object _____
3 frozen _____	4 thrilling _____
5 wriggle _____	6 sunshine _____
7 collect _____	8 crater _____
9 shorten _____	10 decode _____
11 moonlight _____	12 reaches _____
13 review _____	14 gentle _____

Circle and write the two-syllable word that completes each sentence.

15. A planetarium is _____ any theater you've ever seen.

    dislike   unlike   different

16. The ceiling curves over you like a(n) _____ sky.

    endless   ending   dark

17. Stars _____ as though you are really outside.

    shine   wiggle   twinkle

18. The moon and the _____ surround you.

    planets   stars   planes

19. You can watch the _____ of a comet.

    silence   light   movement

20. Meteors go _____ across the sky.

    streak   streaking   streaky

LESSON 115: Assessing Multisyllabic Words

Review this Check-Up with your child.

Have You Ever Seen?

Have you ever seen a sheet on a river bed?
Or a single hair from a hammer's head?
Has the foot of a mountain any toes?
And is there a pair of garden hose?

Does the needle ever wink its eye?
Why doesn't the wing of a building fly?
Can you tickle the ribs of a parasol?
Or open the trunk of a tree at all?

Are the teeth of a rake ever going to bite?
Have the hands of a clock any left or right?
Can the garden plot be deep and dark?
And what is the sound of the birch's bark?

Anonymous

Critical Thinking

How would you answer each question in the poem?

What do you think makes the poem fun to read?

LESSON 116: Synonyms, Antonyms, Homonyms, and Dictionary Skills
Poetry: Word Play and Rhyme

Name _____

Internet
Visit us at
www.sadlier-oxford.com

Dear Family,

In this unit that's just for fun, your child will study words and their meanings. Share these definitions:

synonyms: words that have the same or nearly the same meaning (**sound/noise**)

antonyms: words that have the opposite meaning (**dark/light**)

homonyms: words that sound the same but have different spellings and meanings (**eye/I**)

• Read the poem on the reverse side. Talk about words with more than one meaning, for example, **bed,** and how they make the poem funny.

• Call attention to the rhyming words, such as **bed** and **head.**

• Have fun with words in the poem. Think of a synonym for **seen. (noticed)** Find a pair of antonyms in the last stanza. (**left** and **right**) Think of a homonym for **pair. (pear)**

Apreciada Familia:

En esta unidad que es sólo para divertirse, los niños estudiarán palabras y su significado. Compartan estas definiciones:

sinónimos: palabras que tienen el mismo significado (**sound/noise**)

antónimos: palabras que significan lo opuesto (**dark/light**)

homónimos: palabras que tienen el mismo sonido pero diferente significado y se escriben diferente (**eye/I**)

• Lean el poema en la página 191. Hablen sobre palabras con más de un significado como por ejemplo: **bed,** y como hacen que el poema sea divertido.

• Señale a las palabras que riman tales como: **bed** y **head.**

• Diviértanse con las palabras en el poema. Piensen un sinónimo para **seen. (noticed)** Busque un par de antónimos en la última estrofa. (**left** y **right**) Piensen un homónimo para **pair. (pear)**

PROJECT

Begin a "Word of the Day" campaign. Each day help your child find an unusual word in the dictionary. Write the word on an index card and display it for the day. Encourage your child to use the word in conversation.

Word of the Day: defrost

PROYECTO

Inicie una campaña "Palabra del día". Todos los días ayude al niño a encontrar una palabra poco común en el diccionario. Escriba la palabra en una tarjeta 3 X 5 y exhíbala durante un día. Anime al niño a usar la palabra en una conversación.

Name _____

Helpful Hint **Synonyms** are words that have the same or nearly the same meaning.
rushed—hurried

Draw a line from each word in the first column to its synonym in the second column.

1			2		
rushed	odd		scream	noisy	
start	hurried		loud	spotted	
strange	stay		car	screech	
remain	begin		saw	auto	

3			4		
story	small		center	journey	
large	tune		glad	several	
tiny	huge		few	middle	
song	tale		trip	happy	

Edit each line of the poem. Replace the word in bold print with its synonym from above. Then read the poem.

Last night I looked up and ~~spotted~~ *saw* the moon.

I listened and heard a mysterious **song.**

I **hurried** to the door and what did I see?

A **large** dinosaur was looking at me

And playing a song on a **small** guitar

I'd carelessly left in the family **auto.**

He headed towards me, and I started to **screech.**

That's when I woke up from this very **odd** dream.

Make a list of synonyms for **large** and a list of synonyms for **small.**
Compare lists with your classmates.

Work with a partner to complete the puzzle. Write the synonym from the box for each clue word.

below	city	clever	enjoy	far	forest	frightened
gloomy	go	injure	jog	leap	near	
ocean	oil	pal	ready	reply	rescue	rip

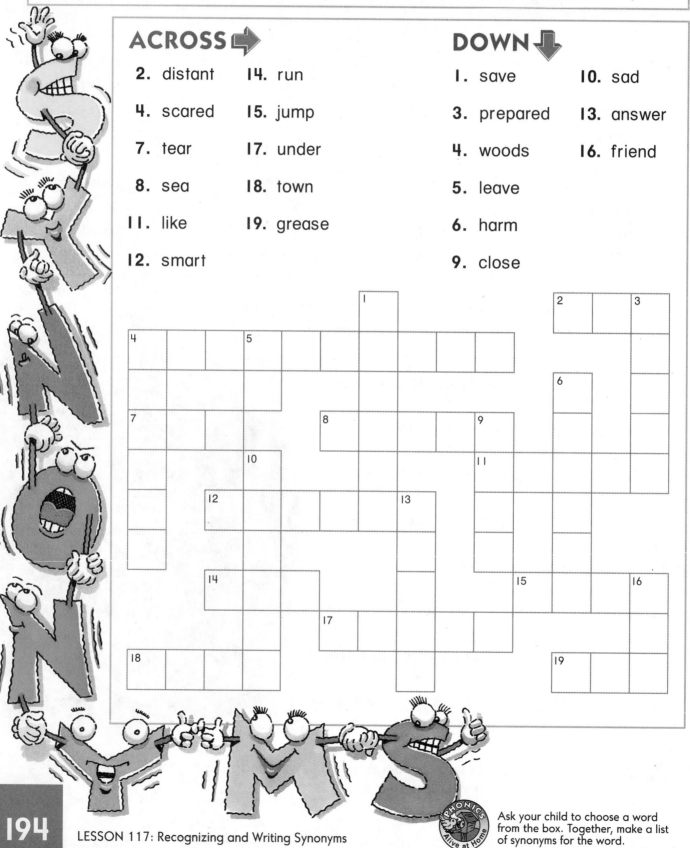

ACROSS ➡

2. distant
4. scared
7. tear
8. sea
11. like
12. smart
14. run
15. jump
17. under
18. town
19. grease

DOWN ⬇

1. save
3. prepared
4. woods
5. leave
6. harm
9. close
10. sad
13. answer
16. friend

LESSON 117: Recognizing and Writing Synonyms

Ask your child to choose a word from the box. Together, make a list of synonyms for the word.

Name _____

Helpful Hint **Antonyms** are words that have the opposite or nearly the opposite meaning.
yesterday—tomorrow

Draw a line from each word in the first column to its antonym in the second column.

1			2		
yesterday	beginning		clean	first	
winter	tomorrow		slowly	early	
end	summer		late	quickly	
empty	full		last	dirty	

3			4		
hello	thin		sharp	none	
come	go		above	dull	
thick	good-bye		all	west	
remember	forget		east	below	

Edit each sentence. Replace the word in bold print with its antonym from above.

5. My alarm didn't ring ~~tomorrow~~. *yesterday*

6. I was afraid I'd be **early** for school.

7. I got dressed **slowly.**

8. I yelled **hello** as I ran out the door.

9. Whew! I was the **last** one at the bus stop.

10. "Don't you **forget**?" Dad called out to me.

11. "Today is the **end** of summer vacation."

12. "**Go** back home!"

Write a message in which you say the opposite of what you mean. Challenge a classmate to use antonyms to decode it.

Write an antonym from the box for each clue word. Then read down to find a tongue twister that answers the question.

after	asleep	cool	daughter	difficult	east	few	healthy
inside	large	neat	old	safe	slow	strong	subtract	tight

1. west _____

2. awake _____

3. messy _____

4. small _____

5. before _____

6. easy _____

7. add _____

8. son _____

9. fast _____

10. loose _____

11. many _____

12. new _____

13. warm _____

14. dangerous _____

15. outside _____

16. weak _____

17. sick _____

What do you call a lobster that won't share?

_____

LESSON 118: Recognizing and Writing Antonyms

At random, ask your child to name an antonym for each clue word in the box at the top.

Helpful Hint **Homonyms** are words that sound the same but have different spellings and meanings.
some—sum

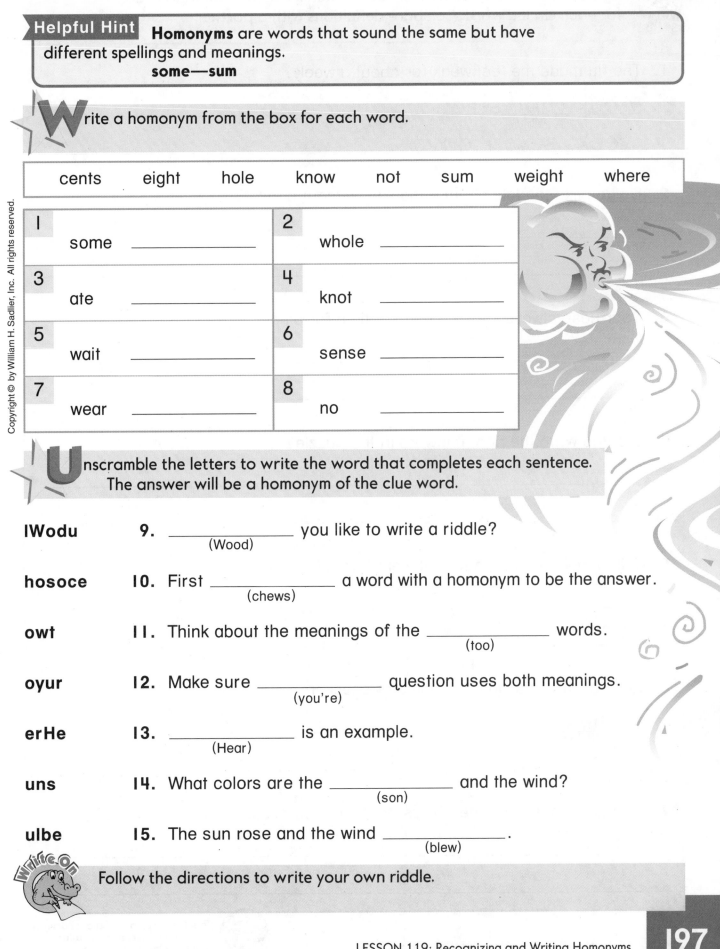

Write a homonym from the box for each word.

cents	eight	hole	know	not	sum	weight	where

1. some _____
2. whole _____
3. ate _____
4. knot _____
5. wait _____
6. sense _____
7. wear _____
8. no _____

Unscramble the letters to write the word that completes each sentence. The answer will be a homonym of the clue word.

lWodu 9. _____ you like to write a riddle? (Wood)

hosoce 10. First _____ a word with a homonym to be the answer. (chews)

owt 11. Think about the meanings of the _____ words. (too)

oyur 12. Make sure _____ question uses both meanings. (you're)

erHe 13. _____ is an example. (Hear)

uns 14. What colors are the _____ and the wind? (son)

ulbe 15. The sun rose and the wind _____. (blew)

Follow the directions to write your own riddle.

Circle the pair of homonyms in each sentence. Then write a definition for each circled word. Compare definitions with a partner.

1. The flu made me feel (weak) for about a (week).

   weak: not strong

   week: seven days

2. Do you like the tale about a monkey without a tail?

   _____

   _____

3. Your nose always knows when it's time for dinner.

   _____

   _____

4. Did you write the right answers in the puzzle?

   _____

   _____

5. Julio threw the ball so hard it went through the window.

   _____

   _____

6. Each of the girls won one game of checkers.

   _____

   _____

7. Dad and Omar rode their bikes on the country road.

   _____

   _____

Together, use each of these homonym pairs in a sentence: **ate, eight; hole, whole; cents, sense.**

Spell, Write, and Tell

Read the phrases in the box. Say and spell each word in bold print. Repeat the word. Then sort the words. Write two pairs of synonyms, two pairs of antonyms, and three pairs of homonyms.

in the **beginning**

dollars and **cents**

a **clever** trick

the **end** of the story

a **hole** in the bucket

inside the house

an **odd** feeling

play **outside**

makes no **sense**

a **smart** dog

a **strange** sound

wagged its **tail**

told a **tale**

ate the **whole** thing

Synonyms

_____ _____

_____ _____

Antonyms

_____ _____

_____ _____

Homonyms

_____ _____

_____ _____

_____ _____

Spell, Write and Tell

Have fun with words. Write a funny story, a silly song, or a rollicking rhyme. Write anything you'd like! Use one or more of your spelling words. Share your work with a friend.

beginning	cents	clever	end	hole	inside	odd
outside	sense	smart	strange	tail	tale	whole

LESSON 120: Connecting Spelling, Writing, and Speaking

PHONICS Alive at Home

Read your child's work. Then write something together. Use one or more spelling words.

Name _____

Read each pair of words. Write S beside synonyms, write A beside antonyms, and write H beside homonyms.

1	quickly—slowly ____	2	would—wood ____
3	loud—noisy ____	4	story—tale ____
5	winter—summer ____	6	eight—ate ____
7	know—no ____	8	empty—full ____
9	rushed—hurried ____	10	threw—through ____
11	won—one ____	12	weight—wait ____
13	tiny—small ____	14	healthy—sick ____
15	remember—forget ____	16	forest—woods ____
17	difficult—easy ____	18	sense—cents ____

Follow the lines and connect the letters to spell synonyms, antonyms, and homonyms. You may start on any letter and move in any direction. Write the words you find.

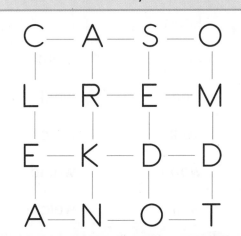

```
C — A   S — O
|   |   |   |
L   R — E   M
|       |   |
E   K   D — D
|   |   |
A — N — O — T
```

19. synonym for **auto** _____

20. homonym for **not** _____

21. antonym for **dirty** _____

22. synonym for **strange** _____

23. homonym for **sum** _____

Check-Up Circle a **synonym** for each word in bold print.

1	**ready**	reading	later	prepared	steady
2	**below**	between	above	behind	under
3	**leap**	jump	loop	fall	frog
4	**scared**	square	frightened	brave	scary
5	**ocean**	raindrop	over	sea	land

Circle an **antonym** for each word in bold print.

6	**safe**	dangerous	safety	bank	protected
7	**weak**	week	small	strong	will
8	**son**	boy	daughter	sun	moon
9	**asleep**	awake	tired	bored	nap
10	**full**	fall	whole	huge	empty

Fill in the circle next to the **homonym** that makes sense in each sentence.

11. I wonder ____ everyone is.   ○ wear   ○ where

12. Don't they ____ it's my birthday?   ○ know   ○ no

13. I'm not ____ years old anymore.   ○ ate   ○ eight

14. I've been waiting patiently for a ____.   ○ weak   ○ week

15. I think I ____ my friends coming now.   ○ hear   ○ here

16. I wish they ____ hurry.   ○ wood   ○ would

17. I can't ____ till they shout "Surprise!"   ○ wait   ○ weight

LESSON 121: Assessing Synonyms, Antonyms, and Homonyms

Review this Check-Up with your child.

Name _____

Read the book review. Think about how the reader felt about the book. Then answer the questions.

Guppies in Tuxedos
by Marvin Terban

Did you know that guppies are named for R. J. Lechmere Guppy? He discovered the fish on a South American island. Formal suits are called tuxedos for Tuxedo Park, New York. That's the place they were first worn.

You will find the story of the words "guppies" and "tuxedos" in Guppies in Tuxedos by Marvin Terban. It's a book of eponyms. An eponym is a person or place that becomes a word.

I was amazed to learn all the words that are eponyms. Leotards are named for a circus performer. Thursday gets its name from Thor, the Scandinavian god of thunder. Hamburgers come from the city of Hamburg in Germany.

My favorite eponym is "teddy" in teddy bear. Believe it or not, "teddy" is Theodore Roosevelt— the 26th president of the United States!

To find out about other eponyms, read Guppies in Tuxedos. You won't be disappointed.

1. What is an eponym?

_____

_____

2. Did the reader enjoy this book? Explain your answer.

_____

_____

Read and Write

Imagine that you are thirty years old, and your name is now a word in the English language. What wonderful or interesting thing have you done? What is named after you? Write the story of your name. Use one or more words from the box.

Writer's Tips

- Choose a category—food, clothing, places, or things—and decide what will be named after you.
- Start by telling what the new word based on your name means.
- Explain how the word came to be named after you.

difficult
easy
forget
hard
hear
here
know
no
quickly
remember
slowly
understand

LESSON 122: Connecting Reading and Writing
Comprehension: Drawing Conclusions

Ask your child to read the story of his or her name. Together, make up a story for your name.

Helpful Hint In a dictionary, words are listed in **alphabetical order.**
apple   banana   coconut   date

Write the missing letters to complete the alphabet. Then write each group of words in alphabetical order.

A___ D___ ___ H___ K___
___ O___ R___ ___ V___ Y___

1

riddle   _____

joke   _____

story   _____

tale   _____

poem   _____

2

piano   _____

music   _____

violin   _____

trumpet   _____

flute   _____

3

laugh   _____

giggle   _____

chuckle   _____

smile   _____

roar   _____

4

you   _____

me   _____

I   _____

we   _____

us   _____

Look at the letter beneath each line. Finish decoding the riddle by writing the next letter in the alphabet.

___ ___ ___ , ___ ___ ___ ___   ___ ___ ___ ___ ___ A ___ ___ ___
V G X   V N M S   D K D O G   M S R

___ ___ ___ ___   ___ ___ ___   ___ ___ ___ ___ ?
D U D Q   F D S   Q H B G

___ ___ A ___   ___ ___ ___   ___ ___ ___ ___
A D B   T R D   S G D X   V N Q J

___ ___ A ___
E N Q   O D M T S R

Write each group of words in alphabetical order.

1		2	
termite	_____	slaw	_____
turtle	_____	stew	_____
toad	_____	shrimp	_____
tadpole	_____	soup	_____
tiger	_____	salad	_____

3		4	
fly	_____	drum	_____
flock	_____	draw	_____
flew	_____	drive	_____
flamingo	_____	drop	_____
flutter	_____	dream	_____

Put each set of words in alphabetical order to write a sentence.
Then take turns reading the sentences with a partner.

5. pizzas made yesterday. Mac pepperoni many

_____

6. big jumped wall. the Angel's over dog

_____

7. twister. the said Maria tongue quickly

_____

Have fun alphabetizing words with your child. Try a grocery list, a book title, a sentence from a book.

Name _____

Helpful Hint **Guide words** are found at the top of each dictionary page. They show the first and last words, or entries, on the page.

peacock/piano
 pea•cock (pē′kok′), a large bird with green, blue, and gold feathers

Read the guide words. Cross out the words that do not belong on the same dictionary page.

1 **peacock/piano**	2 **bloom/bride**	3 **heart/hungry**
panda	book	helpful
phonics	bulldog	high
peacock	better	honor
pelican	bread	hut
peek	blue	hungry

4 **wagon/wind**	5 **light/lucky**	6 **read/roar**
will	loop	ranger
waffle	litter	road
week	lung	rib
wait	low	rule
wish	left	report

Find the path. Go from **Start** to **Finish.** Connect the words that would be found on a dictionary page with guide words **change/coin.**

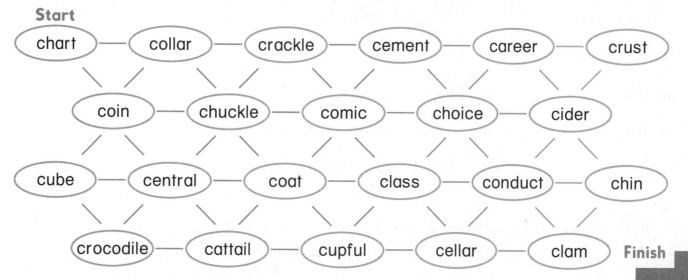

Start

chart — collar — crackle — cement — career — crust

coin — chuckle — comic — choice — cider

cube — central — coat — class — conduct — chin

crocodile — cattail — cupful — cellar — clam   **Finish**

LESSON 124: Using Guide Words

207

snail	share	swan	school	same	sting
slide	subtract	someday	slow	squeal	sash
stamp	secret	sympathy	sky	seal	speak

1 sack/ship

_____

_____

_____

_____

_____

2 six/spoil

_____

_____

_____

_____

_____

3 square/system

_____

_____

_____

_____

_____

Read each sentence. Circle the word that the guide words could help you find in a dictionary.

light/line 4. People have always liked listening to stories.

uncle/unit 5. Stories help us understand our past.

always/another 6. In ancient times Aesop told stories to teach lessons.

table/tease 7. Pioneers told tales around the campfire.

Japan/jewel 8. Kings hired court jesters to tell stories and jokes.

in/inside 9. In western Africa griots had an important job.

heart/houseboat 10. They handed down the history of their people.

Alphabetize each group of words you listed at the top of the page.

Review items 4–10 with your child. Ask your child to explain how he or she completed the exercises.

Name _____

Helpful Hint To quickly find words in a dictionary, turn to the **beginning, middle,** or **end.**

Where in the dictionary would you find the words in the box? Write each word under the correct heading.

laughter	zoo	giggle	noise	humor	knock
delight	jester	yellow	blue	question	wise
funny	silly	television	vitamin	action	octopus

1 Beginning: A–I	**2** Middle: J–Q	**3** End: R–Z
_____	_____	_____
_____	_____	_____
_____	_____	_____
_____	_____	_____
_____	_____	_____

Write **Beginning, Middle,** or **End** to tell where in the dictionary each word in bold print can be found.

4. Sometimes Americans speak in an **unusual** way. _____

5. We say that we "catch a **cold**"—or a train! _____

6. **Sometimes** we "lend a hand"—or an ear. _____

7. **Expressions** like these are called idioms. _____

8. "You're **pulling** my leg" means "you're joking." _____

9. During a **rainstorm,** it's "raining cats and dogs." _____

10. Idioms sound strange, but we know what they **mean.** _____

11. Can you think of an **idiom** you have used? _____

1. pride   _____
   - ○ **press/prince**
   - ○ **phone/piano**
   - ○ **prop/prowl**

2. league   _____
   - ○ **laundry/lay**
   - ○ **lay/lean**
   - ○ **leek/lend**

3. bundle   _____
   - ○ **bullet/bungle**
   - ○ **burst/byte**
   - ○ **bud/bulldog**

4. mob   _____
   - ○ **mistake/moat**
   - ○ **misty/mob**
   - ○ **mock/modern**

5. school   _____
   - ○ **scare/scene**
   - ○ **school/score**
   - ○ **scrape/sea**

6. gaggle   _____
   - ○ **get/giggle**
   - ○ **garden/gear**
   - ○ **gab/game**

7. roundup   _____
   - ○ **river/robot**
   - ○ **root/roundup**
   - ○ **row/rubbish**

8. flock   _____
   - ○ **flesh/flip**
   - ○ **fly/fog**
   - ○ **flock/flute**

9. team   _____
   - ○ **tax/tea**
   - ○ **teen/ten**
   - ○ **taxi/teddy bear**

10. wave   _____
    - ○ **water/wax**
    - ○ **wax/wear**
    - ○ **weak/weave**

11. nest   _____
    - ○ **nest/new**
    - ○ **neck/need**
    - ○ **net/night**

12. collection   _____
    - ○ **circle/clutter**
    - ○ **cobweb/coin**
    - ○ **cocoon/collection**

Ask your child to locate five of the words in a dictionary or to explain how to locate the words.

Name _____

Read the dictionary entries. Then read each sentence and write the number of the entry that tells the meaning of the word in bold print.

> **bark**¹ (bärk), the protective covering of a tree
> **bark**² (bärk), the sound made by a dog

1. My dog will **bark** if a stranger comes near. ____

2. The **bark** of a birch tree is white. ____

> **bat**¹ (bat), a club used to hit the ball in baseball
> **bat**² (bat), a flying mammal

3. If you get the ball, I'll bring the **bat**. ____

4. The **bat** spread its wings and flew off. ____

> **can**¹ (kan), to be able to do something
> **can**² (kan), a metal container for storing something

5. Dad opened a **can** of juice. ____

6. What **can** I do to help you? ____

> **fair**¹ (fer), giving the same treatment to everyone
> **fair**² (fer), a showing of farm goods

7. A judge must always be **fair**. ____

8. My pig won first prize at the county **fair**. ____

> **story**¹ (stôr´ē), a tale of some events
> **story**² (stôr´ē), the rooms on one level of a building

9. Keisha's room is on the second **story**. ____

10. That was the best **story** I ever read! ____

clip[1] (klip), to cut
clip[2] (klip), to attach or fasten

1. You can use these scissors to **clip** the coupons. ____

2. Please **clip** the papers together. ____

fan[1] (fan), a machine that moves air
fan[2] (fan), a person who strongly admires something

3. A true baseball **fan** hates to miss a game. ____

4. If the room gets warm, turn on the **fan.** ____

match[1] (mach), a short piece of wood or cardboard used for lighting a fire
match[2] (mach), to be the same or go together

5. Use a **match** to light the candles. ____

6. Look for curtains that **match** the carpet. ____

rare[1] (rer), unusual
rare[2] (rer), not cooked for very long

7. Snow is **rare** in this part of the country. ____

8. I cooked the meat longer because it was too **rare.** ____

stable[1] (stā′bəl), a building where horses are kept
stable[2] (stā′bəl), firm or steady

9. This old chair is not **stable.** ____

10. Michael led the pony back to the **stable.** ____

Look up the word **shed** in the dictionary. How many entries do you find? Write a sentence for each entry.

Choose a pair of homographs. Together, write a new sentence for each word in the pair.

Name _____

If a word has more than one meaning, it will have more than one dictionary definition.

Read the dictionary entry. Then read each sentence and write the number of the definition that tells the meaning of the word in bold print.

---

foot (fu̇t), **1** the end of a leg **2** the lowest part

1. Julia kicked the ball with her **foot.** ____

2. Jake left his backpack near the **foot** of the stairs. ____

---

head (hed), **1** the upper part of the body where the eyes, ears, nose, mouth, and brain are **2** the striking or cutting part of a tool

3. I wear a hat on my **head** when I go out in the sun. ____

4. I hit my thumb with the **head** of the hammer. ____

---

plot (plot), **1** the events in a story **2** a small piece of ground

5. I set aside a **plot** for a vegetable garden. ____

6. The **plot** was so exciting that I couldn't put down the book. ____

---

trunk (trungk), **1** the main stem of a tree **2** a large box with a lid

7. The **trunk** of that sequoia tree is very wide. ____

8. Let me help you pack your **trunk.** ____

---

wing (wing), **1** the part of an animal's body used for flying **2** a part that sticks out from the main part of a building

9. The park ranger helped a bird with an injured **wing.** ____

10. The gym is in the new **wing** of the school. ____

beam (bēm), **1** a long, large piece of wood or metal **2** a ray of light

1. The **beam** of the flashlight lit the way. ____

2. The carpenter nailed the **beam** in place. ____

cast (kast), **1** the actors in a show **2** a stiff dressing or mold used to hold a broken bone in place

3. When the play was over, the **cast** came out on stage. ____

4. The doctor put a **cast** on Ariel's broken arm. ____

check (chek), **1** a mark made to show that something is correct or has been noted **2** a slip of paper showing how much is owed for a restaurant meal

5. The waiter brought the **check** to the table. ____

6. The teacher put a **check** next to each correct answer. ____

deck (dek), **1** the floor of a ship **2** a pack of playing cards

7. Captain Jack ordered the sailors to wash the **deck**. ____

8. The magician asked me to pick a card from the **deck**. ____

model (mod´əl), **1** a small copy of something **2** a person whose job it is to wear clothing or makeup that is for sale

9. The **model** wore a blue suit. ____

10. Adam built a **model** of an airplane. ____

screen (skrēn), **1** the surface on which a movie is projected **2** wire netting

11. The **screen** on the window keeps flies out. ____

12. This theater has a wide **screen**. ____

Choose one of the dictionary entries. Together, write a new sentence for each definition.

Name _____

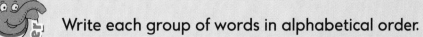

Write each group of words in alphabetical order.

1

run   _____

touchdown _____

goal   _____

basket   _____

point   _____

2

orange   _____

grape   _____

lime   _____

lemon   _____

cherry   _____

3

monkey   _____

leopard   _____

zebra   _____

lion   _____

giraffe   _____

4

Trent   _____

Trisha   _____

Truman   _____

Tracy   _____

Troy   _____

Read the guide words. Circle the words that belong on the same dictionary page.

5   idea/inch

ignore
impossible
ice
imagine
index

6   zero/zoo

zone
zoom
zipper
zebra
zigzag

7   panda/pass

parade
pancake
patch
paper
partner

8   fix/fold

fish
flag
flea
focus
fox

9   near/next

neigh
nice
navy
news
need

10   dancer/decide

dare
deal
daylight
damp
deed

Help explain each riddle by writing two definitions for each word in bold print.

What can you use to mend a broken watermelon?
A watermelon **patch**!

1. _____

2. _____

I have **eyes,** but I can't see. What am I?
A potato.

3. _____

4. _____

I have three **feet,** but no toes. What am I?
A yardstick.

5. _____

6. _____

Why is a baseball game like a pancake?
They both need the **batter.**

7. _____

8. _____

What do you **serve,** but never eat?
A tennis ball!

9. _____

10. _____

LESSON 128: Reviewing Dictionary Skills

Together, make up riddles based on these words with more than one meaning: **bark, trunk, wing, head.**

Name _____

Look and Learn

Let's read and talk about the different uses of some English words.

Imagine your family is going to drive through England this summer. The following tips from an English auto club may help you plan ahead.

1. Pack the **boot** of the **auto** carefully.
2. Keep a litterbag in the front for potato **crisp** bags and other snack wrappers.
3. Before your trip, stop at a **petrol** station. Ask the worker to lift the **bonnet** and check the oil.
4. If a big **lorry** suddenly **overtakes** you, don't cut off the driver. You don't want to get a dent in the **wing.**

What synonyms would you use for the words in bold print?

Do you know of other terms or phrases that are used differently in another country or in another section of the United States?

LESSON 129: Synonyms, Antonyms, Homonyms, and Dictionary Skills in Context
Comprehension: Comparing and Contrasting

217

Check-Up Read the guide words. Cross out the word that does not belong on the same dictionary page. Then write the remaining words in alphabetical order.

1

vary/violin

vase

violet _____

vest _____

vine _____

valentine _____

2

leave/lump

litterbug

lucky _____

lunch _____

lime _____

leave _____

3

eight/empty

elbow

empty _____

eel _____

eight _____

election _____

4

waltz/wise

within

weekend _____

whistle _____

water _____

web _____

Read each sentence. Fill in the circle next to the correct meaning of the word in bold print.

5. What will you **serve** at your party?

   ○ offer to others   ○ put a ball into play

6. The **story** you told made me laugh.

   ○ tale about events   ○ level of a building

7. Can you thread the needle, or is the **eye** too small?

   ○ body part by which you see   ○ hole in a needle

8. What's the **plot** of the book?

   ○ main story   ○ piece of ground

9. Lucky's **bark** is loud, but he doesn't bite.

   ○ tree covering   ○ sound a dog makes

10. Let me show you around the school's new **wing.**

   ○ animal part used for flying   ○ part of the building

Review this Check-Up with your child.

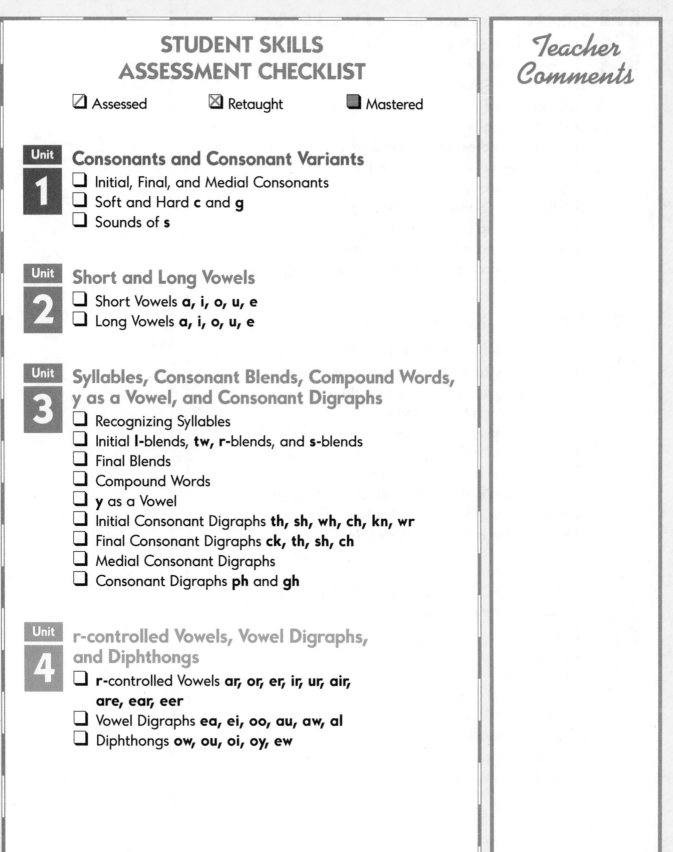

STUDENT SKILLS
ASSESSMENT CHECKLIST

☑ Assessed   ☒ Retaught   ▣ Mastered

Unit 1

Consonants and Consonant Variants
❑ Initial, Final, and Medial Consonants
❑ Soft and Hard **c** and **g**
❑ Sounds of **s**

Unit 2

Short and Long Vowels
❑ Short Vowels **a, i, o, u, e**
❑ Long Vowels **a, i, o, u, e**

Unit 3

Syllables, Consonant Blends, Compound Words, y as a Vowel, and Consonant Digraphs
❑ Recognizing Syllables
❑ Initial **l**-blends, **tw**, **r**-blends, and **s**-blends
❑ Final Blends
❑ Compound Words
❑ **y** as a Vowel
❑ Initial Consonant Digraphs **th, sh, wh, ch, kn, wr**
❑ Final Consonant Digraphs **ck, th, sh, ch**
❑ Medial Consonant Digraphs
❑ Consonant Digraphs **ph** and **gh**

Unit 4

r-controlled Vowels, Vowel Digraphs, and Diphthongs
❑ **r**-controlled Vowels **ar, or, er, ir, ur, air, are, ear, eer**
❑ Vowel Digraphs **ea, ei, oo, au, aw, al**
❑ Diphthongs **ow, ou, oi, oy, ew**

Teacher Comments

Unit 5 — Syllables, Contractions, and Word Endings

- ❑ Recognizing Syllables in Multisyllabic Words
- ❑ Words Ending in **le**
- ❑ Words with Schwa
- ❑ Contractions
- ❑ Plural Endings **s** and **es**
- ❑ Adding **s** and **es** to Words Ending in **y**
- ❑ Adding **es** to Words Ending in **f** and **fe**
- ❑ Singular and Plural Possessives
- ❑ Inflectional Endings **s, es, ing, ed**
- ❑ Changing **y** to **i** Before Adding **es** or **ed**
- ❑ Dropping Final **e** Before Adding **ing** or **ed**
- ❑ Doubling Final Consonant Before Adding **ing** or **ed**

Unit 6 — Suffixes, Prefixes, and Multisyllabic Words

- ❑ Suffixes **ful, less, ness, ly, y, er, est**
- ❑ Suffixes **en, able, ible, ment, ion, er, or, ist**
- ❑ Prefixes **re, un, dis, in, im, pre, de, mis**
- ❑ Syllabication in VCCV Words
- ❑ Syllabication in VCV Words
- ❑ Syllabication in Compound Words
- ❑ Syllabication in Words Ending in **le**
- ❑ Syllabication in Words with Inflectional Endings
- ❑ Syllabication in Words with Suffixes
- ❑ Syllabication in Words with Prefixes

Unit 7 — Synonyms, Antonyms, Homonyms, and Dictionary Skills

- ❑ Synonyms
- ❑ Antonyms
- ❑ Homonyms
- ❑ Alphabetical Order
- ❑ Using Guide Words
- ❑ Locating Words
- ❑ Homographs
- ❑ Multiple Meanings

Name _____

An Amazing Birthday Game

Let me introduce myself. My name is Jack, and my sister's name is Mary. Our father is the gardener for the Duke and Duchess of Beltrain. I became friendly with their son, Harry. He invited Mary and me to his tenth birthday party. I thought the party would be boring, but I had quite an adventure.

Fold

Help Jack and Harry find their way out of the maze. Then write your own ending for the story.

Directions: Cut and fold the book.

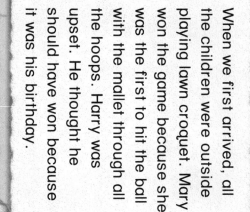

2

When we first arrived, all the children were outside playing lawn croquet. Mary won the game because she was the first to hit the ball with the mallet through all the hoops. Harry was upset. He thought he should have won because it was his birthday.

Fold

3

I wanted to help Harry win one game. I suggested we be partners in finding our way through the new garden maze my father had made. Well, we were the only ones to find our way to the center, but we couldn't find our way back out. Night was falling, and we were starting to panic.

Name _____

A Laugh a Day!

What's your favorite kind of joke? Do you like to hear or tell knock-knocks, riddles, or puns? Do jokes help you to think about words in a new way? See which kind of joke in this book seems the funniest to you. Remember: It's important to laugh at least once a day!

Fold

Puns

It's raining cats and dogs outside!
I know. I just stepped in a poodle.

I saw a catfish yesterday.
Really? How did it hold the pole?

Write the funniest joke you know. Remember to share it with someone who needs a laugh.

_____
_____
_____
_____
_____

4

Directions: Cut and fold the book.

Units 5–7 Take-Home Book
Comprehension: Determining Author's Purpose

Knock-Knock Jokes

Make sure you read these aloud.

Knock, knock.
Who's there?
Tuba.
Tuba who?
Tuba toothpaste.

Knock, knock.
Who's there?
Orange.
Orange who?
Orange you glad
I came to see ya'?

Knock, knock.
Who's there?
Pizza.
Pizza who?
Pizza 'fraid of
scary movies.

Fold

Riddles

Ha! Ha! Ha!

Why do birds fly south for
the winter?
They can't afford to take the train.

What kind of deer carry umbrellas?
Reindeer!

What coat is usable only when it's wet?
A coat of paint!

Where do fish keep their life savings?
In a river bank!

BANK

3

Units 5–7 Take-Home Book
Comprehension: Determining Author's Purpose